LIBERTY, EQUALITY, AND FRATERNITY

Organized by The Wolfsonian–
Florida International University,
Miami Beach, Florida,
from the Centre national
des arts plastiques, France

Curatorial team:
matali crasset
Marianne Lamonaca
M/M (Paris)
Alexandra Midal

Edited by Marianne Lamonaca

With essays by
Marianne Lamonaca
Alexandra Midal
Emilia Philippot

The Wolfsonian–
Florida International University,
Miami Beach, Florida

The Wolfsonian
FLORIDA INTERNATIONAL UNIVERSITY

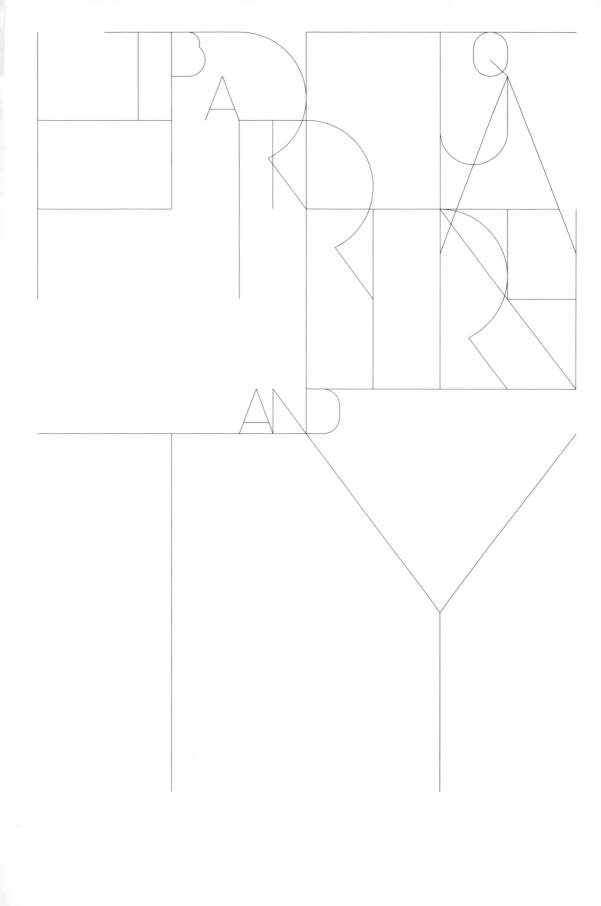

Designed at M/M (Paris)

Copy editor: Andrea Gollin

Special thanks to Wolfsonian
colleagues, Matthew Abess,
Lisa Li, Jonathan Mogul,
and Ivana Rodriguez,
and translators Earlywn Covington
(Alexandra Midal essay)
and Roselyne Pirson
(Emilia Philippot essay)
for their participation in the editing
and production of this volume.

The Wolfsonian–
Florida International University
1001 Washington Avenue
Miami Beach, Florida 33139
USA

www.wolfsonian.org

The Wolfsonian
FLORIDA INTERNATIONAL UNIVERSITY

LIBERTY, EQUALITY, AND FRATERNITY
is sponsored by Van Cleef & Arpels;
Centre national des arts plastiques, France;
and Institut français. Additional support
received from Crédit Agricole Private
Banking Miami; Services Culturels de
l'Ambassade de France/Maison Française;
Funding Arts Network; United Airlines,
the Official Airline of The Wolfsonian–FIU;
Wolfsonian Visionaries; Northern Trust;
Furthermore: a program of the J.M. Kaplan
Fund; and the South Beach Group Hotels.

All works in this publication are in
the collection of the Centre national
des arts plastiques, France.

Printed in Iceland by Oddi Printing.

Library of Congress Cataloging-
in-Publication Data

Liberty, equality, and fraternity /
edited by Marianne Lamonaca ; with
essays by Marianne Lamonaca, Emilia
Philippot, Alexandra Midal. -- 1st ed.
    p. cm.
    Published to accompany an exhibition
organized by the Wolfsonian-Florida
International University from the Centre
national des arts plastiques, France,
to be held at the Wolfsonian-Florida
International University, Miami Beach,
Fla., Nov. 25, 2011-Mar. 26, 2012.
    ISBN 978-0-9677359-4-8 (pbk.)
    1. Design--France--History--20th century-
-Exhibitions. 2. Design--France--History--
21st century--Exhibitions. 3. Design--Political
aspects--France--Exhibitions. 4. National
characteristics, French, in art--Exhibitions.
5. Centre national des arts plastiques
(France)--Exhbitions. I. Lamonaca, Marianne.
II. Philippot, Emilia. III. Midal, Alexandra. IV.
Wolfsonian-Florida International University. V.
Centre national des arts plastiques (France)
    NK1449.A1L53 2011
    745.0944'0904--dc23
                            2011040822

Published by The Wolfsonian–
Florida International University to
accompany the exhibition
LIBERTY, EQUALITY, AND FRATERNITY,
organized by The Wolfsonian–FIU
from the Centre national des arts plastiques,
France, held 25 November 2011–26
March 2012 at The Wolfsonian–FIU,
Miami Beach, Florida.

FOREWORD
Cathy Leff
Director, The Wolfsonian–FIU

In 2009 Gaël de Maisonneuve, Consul General of the Consulate General of France in Miami, and Norbert Duffort, the Consulate's Cultural Attaché, facilitated the introduction of The Wolfsonian–Florida International University to Anne-Marie Charbonneaux, President, Centre national des arts plastiques (National Center for Visual Arts, or CNAP), and Richard Lagrange, CNAP's director. That meeting initiated a relationship—and now, friendship—that resulted in the exhibition, LIBERTY, EQUALITY, AND FRATERNITY, and its accompanying publication.

The CNAP, created in 1982, oversees a national patrimony that includes decorative and design arts, mostly of the post-war era. This patrimony has been shared with the French public from its inception, through museum loans and CNAP-curated projects presented mostly in that nation's cultural venues. When the CNAP approached The Wolfsonian, and specifically Marianne Lamonaca, our Associate Director for Curatorial Affairs and Education, with an invitation to curate and present an exhibition, it was the first time a non-French museum had been asked and given a free reign to develop a project. Looking at this material through the lens of The Wolfsonian has been an exciting and enriching experience for all involved, and one that we are thrilled to share with the public.

Like the CNAP, The Wolfsonian has a vast and varied patrimony of decorative and design arts, although our collection is chiefly from the late nineteenth to mid-twentieth centuries. We are known for our multidisciplinary approach in which the art and design of everyday life are considered in the context of the social, political, and technological forces that shaped their creation, and as active agents in human affairs. As part of that narrative, national and cultural identity is a strong *leitmotif* of The Wolfsonian's holdings. This emphasis on contextual identity is readily evident in many areas within the collection: the "Romantic Nationalism" of early twentieth-century Scandinavian design; government-sponsored public art and architecture programs, such as New Deal post office murals; and graphic design used to promote national identity in Germany in the late-nineteenth and early-twentieth centuries, to cite just a few examples.

It thus seemed so "Wolfsonian" when our chief curator chose the French motto "liberté, égalité, fraternité" as a framework for examining how a nation's patrimony and a selection of French design objects within it expressed the country's cultural and national identity. It further seemed so characteristic of our curatorial approach to ensure that all aspects of the project reflect what it means to be French, and more specifically, how the nation's ideals are manifest in its contemporary cultural production. This could not have been achieved without identifying an interdisciplinary team of talented design professionals with whom to engage in thinking about French design and its underlying political and cultural relevance, and also in having that team then participate in the project design.

The resulting exhibition and publication represent a dynamic collaboration between France-based design professionals matali crasset, M/M Paris (Michael Amzalag and Mathias Augustyniak), and Alexandra Midal, and The Wolfsonian's Marianne Lamonaca and Richard Miltner, Exhibition Designer. In addition, we thank Francis Fichot of matali crasset productions.

I am exceedingly grateful to the curatorial and design team—with its cast of such distinguished designers and design historians—for working together despite challenging deadlines, difficult time zones, and cultural and language differences to create a rich and textured understanding of post-war French design.

I also want to recognize Wolfsonian colleagues Matthew Abess, Kimberly Bergen, Donna Carter, Julieth Dabdoub, Steve Forero-Paz, Lisa Li, Jonathan Mogul, Mylinh Nguyen, Whitney Richardson, Ivana Rodriguez, and Amy Silverman, for their important contributions. The publication was strengthened by Andrea Gollin's careful review of the manuscript.

This effort would not have been possible without the initial invitation from and financial support of our CNAP partners—Anne-Marie Charbonneaux and Richard Lagrange. I thank them for the opportunity to engage in this wonderful international collaboration and for their confidence and trust in our work. I commend the entire CNAP team for their participation, especially Claude Allemand-Cosneau, Emilia Philippot, Aude Bodet, Christelle Demoussis, Danielle Catherine, and Bénédicte Godin.

Fundamental to our ability to mount an ambitious show was the generous funding we received from the Institut français. I am particularly grateful to Max Moulin, Head of Museum, Exhibitions and Design Service; and Alain Reinaudo, Advisor for the Visual Arts and Architecture, Deputy Director, for backing this project from its inception.

The Miami presentation of LIBERTY, EQUALITY, AND FRATERNITY and the accompanying publication would not have been possible without the commitment of Nicolas Bos, President and CEO of the Americas, and the generous sponsorship of Van Cleef & Arpels.

Additional and critical funding was provided by Crédit Agricole Private Banking Miami. We also recognize Services Culturels de l'Ambassade de France/Maison Française; Funding Arts Network; United Airlines, the Official Airline of The Wolfsonian–FIU; the Wolfsonian Visionaries; Northern Trust; Furthermore: a program of the J.M. Kaplan Fund; and South Beach Group Hotels for their generosity and support.

I thank Wolfsonian friends and advisors from the Consulate General of France in Miami for bringing this project to us, especially Gaël de Maisonneuve, Consul General; Norbert Duffort, Cultural Attaché; and Kimberley Gaultier, Deputy Attaché: Arts et culture. I appreciate the advice of our Paris-based friends Jill Silverman, Galerie Thaddaeus Ropac; Didier Krzentowski, Galerie Kreo; Béatrice Salmon, Les Arts Décoratifs; Françoise Guichon, Centre Pompidou; and Cathy Vedovi.

We continue to be inspired by the vision of Wolfsonian founder Mitchell Wolfson, Jr., who infused into our institutional identity a curiosity and commitment to explore the concept "what man makes, makes man," which prepared us to undertake a project whose scope might be unexpected for the Wolfsonian.

FOREWORD
Richard Lagrange,
Director, Centre national des arts plastiques
Sylviane Tarsot-Gillery,
Executive Director, Institut français

When Norbert Duffort, Cultural Attaché at the Consulate General of France in Miami, introduced us to the museum in 2009, we were immediately seduced by The Wolfsonian, by its space and its highly original collection that takes in an extraordinary variety of fields. Naturally then, we were enthused by the idea of giving carte blanche to Marianne Lamonaca, Associate Director for Curatorial Affairs and Education at The Wolfsonian, to curate an exhibition from the design collection of the Centre national des arts plastiques (CNAP) that would focus on French design.

The CNAP is another singular and original institution whose collection, open to artists from all over the world, covers a wide range of expressions: painting, sculpture, installation, performance art, photography, video, graphic design, decorative art, and design. More than six thousand objects comprise the CNAP's design collection, acquired over a period of thirty years. The collection clearly conveys the diversity of international creation in the applied arts and design. The collection ranges in scope from furniture, light fittings, tableware, and textiles to, on a more modest scale, jewelry, domestic appliances, hi-fi, and fashion. Through regular acquisitions, the CNAP records the most representative currents and trends of its times. The result is a collection that traces the evolution of creation over the past three decades, and highlights the changing relationships between the various people in the production chain (designer, manufacturer, distributor).

The Institut français supports exhibitions of established or emerging designers as well as educational exchanges between prestigious French universities and their foreign counterparts. Beginning in 2000, design has become an increasingly important area of concentration for the Institut français.

While The Wolfsonian's collection includes works from several European countries, France seems less represented. This exhibition, which presents an American museum's perspective on French design, allows for a remarkable journey through a wide field of creation, and showcases the talent of our country's designers. Marianne Lamonaca has brought together some one hundred and twenty-five objects, including works by Pierre Paulin, Olivier Mourgue, Jean Royère, the Bouroullec brothers, Roger Tallon, and Philippe Starck. She has enlisted foremost French designers matali crasset and M/M Paris (Michael Amzalag and Mathias Augustyniak) for the exhibition design, and Alexandra Midal, a historian and theorist of design, to elaborate on the point of view developed in the exhibition within the catalogue.

The CNAP, as part of its mission to promote contemporary artistic creation, wishes to encourage the widest possible dissemination of the works it acquires on behalf of the French state, both in France and internationally. We would therefore like to thank The Wolfsonian for its participation, about which the CNAP and the Institut français are delighted. Our wish is that this exhibition introduce an American and international audience to the work of our most talented designers. Presented during the time of Art Basel Miami Beach 2011, LIBERTY, EQUALITY, AND FRATERNITY enjoys the support of the French Embassy in the United States. It has been a hugely satisfying experience to design and produce this exhibition with the people who have become our friends at The Wolfsonian in Miami Beach.

INTRODUCTION

Marianne Lamonaca,
Associate Director for Curatorial Affairs
and Education, The Wolfsonian–FIU

For centuries France has held a central place as an arbiter of style and taste. The role of the French court in establishing art, architecture, design, and craftsmanship as essential signifiers of French identity has a long, storied history. A visit to the Louvre or Versailles will make that clear. The French also have an extensive tradition of supporting the applied arts. During the reign of Louis XIV in the seventeenth century, workshops were established (some still in existence today) to produce interior decoration, furnishings, and other decorative items, such as porcelain, silver tableware, and tapestries for use at royal properties throughout France. Today, the Ministry of Culture and Communication continues the government's role as a patron of the arts in many ways. Of particular note for decorative art and craft is the program that oversees the commissioning of new works to be produced at the legendary French manufactures at Sèvres (porcelain), the Mobilier national (furniture), and Gobelins (textiles). The Ministry also supports the acquisition, presentation, and preservation of decorative art, craft, and industrial design through the Centre national des arts plastiques (National Center for Visual Arts, or CNAP). Established in 1982, the CNAP was one of the important cultural programs put in place during the presidency of François Mitterrand (1981–1994), France's first Socialist president. The CNAP collects in the area of visual arts, photography, and decorative art, craft, and industrial design, and is charged with collecting, preserving, and disseminating the collection throughout France and abroad.

Norbert Duffort, Cultural Attaché at the Consulate General of France in Miami, suggested that The Wolfsonian curate and mount a show from the CNAP collection. His enlightened matchmaking recognized that The Wolfsonian's mission—the study and appreciation of the "persuasive power of art and design"—and its curatorial approach—to explore the contexts in which objects are made and disseminated—would provide a fresh framework for understanding the decorative art, craft, and design collection of the CNAP.

Presented with the prospect of curating an exhibition from the CNAP, I began to research its history and the composition of its collection. The collection of more than six thousand objects is comprised of artifacts of French origin as well as those from other countries. In the early 1980s, for example, important works by the Milanese-based Memphis group were acquired, and more recently works by the Dutch design collective Droog. As I considered my curatorial approach, I found myself drawn to the essential fact that the French government annually purchases design objects for the national patrimony. The works are catalogued, photographed, and made available to the public through an online database. The CNAP is entrusted with the responsibility of making the collection available for exhibitions or for long-term loan to museums and art centers throughout France. This commitment to the dissemination of the collection is very important, and is, in fact, the foundation of the collaboration with The Wolfsonian.

After reviewing the collection, I decided to explore the CNAP materials as an expression of the intersection of design and politics in France, focusing on French decorative art, craft, and design alone. I based my decision on several criteria: the CNAP itself, with its central role of collecting for the nation, was born as a political act; the history of French decorative art, craft, and design from the post-war era to today has been shaped and supported by French cultural policies; the presentation of works made only in France would help define the collection for a non-French audience; and more than twenty years have passed since twentieth-century French decorative arts have been the focus of a large exhibition in the United States.[1] Together, these considerations informed my decision to use the French motto, "liberté, égalité, fraternité," as the interpretive framework for the show. Conveying the ideals of the new republic, the motto first appeared during the French Revolution, itself an expression of the Age of Enlightenment. It reflects the growing awareness and defense of democratic values, in particular, popular sovereignty, and the individual's right to liberty and equality under the law. In 1880 when the French declared July 14th—the day on which the Bastille fell in 1789—a national holiday, the motto was widely accepted. It later appeared as a foundational element in the French constitutions of 1946 and 1958, and is widely used today on items such as coins and postage stamps.

For me, the very existence of the CNAP is proof of the motto's continued relevance, as reflected in the shared belief that French national culture should be supported and enriched by the government for the people of France. The CNAP collection, along with countless other state-sponsored cultural and educational initiatives, has a role to play in communicating a common public culture to the nation, as well as in shaping the public perception of France throughout the world.

LIBERTY, EQUALITY, AND FRATERNITY will be on view at the time of two significant contemporary art fairs: Art Basel Miami Beach and Design Miami. From the outset, I envisioned creating an experience for visitors (including those who travel to Miami primarily for the fairs) that would enlighten them about French design history, but would also provide the occasion for contemporary French designers to present their work within an historical continuum. With my curatorial concept in place, I invited a team of partners to work with me to shape the exhibition narrative, select objects, and contribute to and design the exhibition and publication. Design historian and theorist Alexandra Midal along with designers matali crasset, Michael Amzalag, and Mathias Augustyniak shared their perceptions and knowledge about the CNAP, French design history and practice, and French culture and politics. From different backgrounds and disciplines, they each offered their highly personal knowledge and interpretations of the material presented. I relished their spirited discussions about French cultural policy, noting, at times, their personal dissatisfaction with the national design landscape; found inspiration in their deep knowledge of and reverence for French culture, from film to literature, from popular culture to political thought; and was amused by inside jokes, including some with scatological and sexual connotations.

LIBERTY, EQUALITY, AND FRATERNITY investigates the expressive ability of design objects to embody concrete and symbolic ideas expressed by the French national motto. The exhibition and accompanying publication are based on the principle that objects have agency, that they impact the world in which we live, and that they can tell stories about the context in which they were made. Together, the curatorial framework, the objects on view, and the design of the exhibition and publication provide a vibrant and complex narrative of French design from the 1940s to today.

More than one hundred objects were selected for the exhibition. My hope is that the energy, commitment, and creativity that have gone into conceiving the project and selecting these representative objects will lead to a growing awareness of and interest in French innovation, craftsmanship, and personal expression among those who view the exhibition and read the catalogue. I also anticipate that showcasing this material beyond the borders of France will foster new opportunities for bringing this important French collection to an ever-growing public.

Many people have made this project a reality, from our French design collaborators (Michael Amzalag, Mathias Augustyniak, matali crasset, and Alexandra Midal) and the staff of the CNAP, to my generous Wolfsonian colleagues. I especially want to acknowledge the assistance of Matthew Abess, Donna Carter, Julieth Dabdoub, Andrea Gollin, Cathy Leff, Lisa Li, Richard Miltner, and Jonathan Mogul.

THE PUBLICATION
This volume presents three essays that situate French design within an historical framework. Each explores the subject of national identity and design in a different way. My essay, "Liberty, Equality and Fraternity: A Dialog with Ordinary Things," offers an overview of French design history over the past sixty years. The piece gives the reader a context for understanding the role that politics plays in shaping design production and consumption. The decade-by-decade narrative touches upon key political, cultural, and economic circumstances that have shaped design culture in France, using examples from the collection of the CNAP.

Emilia Philippot, heritage curator of decorative art, craft, and industrial design at the CNAP, provides a condensed history of the CNAP and its collection. Her focus is on the important role the CNAP plays in linking together culture and national identity through its collection policies and its programs of dissemination. Philippot enlightens the reader about the formation of the CNAP, its roots that go back to the Revolutionary era, and the nature of its program and collection. In the service of national culture, the CNAP continues the centuries-long tradition of state patronage of art in France.

A visual essay presents the nine narrative clusters of the exhibition:

1   FRENCH DESIGN DIGEST—The Framework
2   STARCK SYSTEM—The Star
3   DREAM PRODUCTS—The Sandwich Material
4   FRENCH ADMINISTRATION—The Pediment
5   CITY OF THE MIND—The Tree
6   AN IDEAL HOME—Forming a Circle
7   ARMCHAIR ACTIVIST—The Barricade
8   ALPHA-OMEGA—Model for a City
9   MIXED MEDIA—The Chain

Conceived as a series of portraits, each cluster expresses an important theme, personality, or context. Collectively, they propose a novel reading of French design history from the 1940s to today.

The final essay "Dial D for Design," by design historian and theorist Alexandra Midal, proposes her own critical re-writing of French design history. Reflecting on the choice of the French motto as the show's conceptual framework, Midal takes up the theme of the political agency of design objects. Assuming the role of detective, she offers a narrative that unfolds like a criminal investigation. The crime in question takes place on the contested terrain of design history. Midal's essay weaves together aspects of Walter Benjamin's peculiar materialism, Barthes's "mythologies," Georges Bataille's violence of form, as well as countless other literary and film references in order to reveal what she posits as the accursed history of design, and to metaphorically "murder" it.

—

Notes

1. Conceived as part of France's bicentennial celebration, the exhibition and accompanying publication, *L'Art de vivre*, at the Cooper-Hewitt Museum in 1989, cast a wide net highlighting French decorative arts from 1789 to 1989.

LIBERTY, EQUALITY, AND FRATERNITY:
A DIALOG WITH ORDINARY THINGS
Marianne Lamonaca

French decorative arts and design of the twentieth century can be characterized by two important episodes that cemented France's role as the arbiter of style and taste in the first part of the 1900s: the Exposition universelle of 1900, where Art Nouveau's organic forms were presented alongside the monuments of the new industrialism, the Tour Eiffel (1889), and Hector Guimard's metro stations; and the Exposition internationale des arts décoratifs et industriels modernes of 1925, where the House of the Collector by *ebéniste* Emile-Jacques Ruhlmann, epitomizing the luxurious and beautifully crafted modern style known today as Art Deco, shared the stage with architect Le Corbusier's Pavillon de l'esprit nouveau, a defiant expression of the machine and standardization. The marketplace for interior decoration, furniture, and small decorative arts was served by a very complex and sophisticated group of makers centered around producers—such as *ébénistes* working in wood and *artistes décorateurs* with their roots in the trade guilds and the royal manufactures of past centuries. Professional organizations such as the Société des artistes décorateurs (founded in 1901) promoted French craftsmanship and luxury goods through its annual Salon. The Union des artistes modernes (UAM) was formed in 1929 to promote design for mass production, at a time when the industrial infrastructure did not exist in France. Le Corbusier, Charlotte Perriand, and René Herbst were among its principal members. Like other nations in Europe at the time, France struggled to balance its national traditions with modernity and internationalism. It embraced the machine, while nurturing craft production; broadened its market from a wealthy elite to a wider public; and put into place cultural and economic policies to support decorative art and design. France further reinforced its status as a modern world leader in culture and politics at two large exhibitions in the 1930s: the Exposition coloniale in 1931, showcasing the nation's political and economic might, and the Exposition internationale des arts et techniques dans la vie moderne in 1937, focusing on technological progress.

The Second World War, of course, interrupted these developments. When it ended, the enormous task of rebuilding began. Through the program popularly known as the Marshall Plan, the U.S. poured millions of dollars into reconstruction, vocational training, and food programs. France's strong traditions of agriculture, craftsmanship, and industry were the keys to its success. The period of economic and population growth in France that began in 1945 and ended around the time of the international oil crisis in 1973 is referred to as the "glorious thirty" (*les trentes glorieuses*). It was also marked by profound social changes that impacted education, social welfare, and culture.

Decorators like Jean Royère continued to produce stylish furnishings for an upper-class clientele. In a chair he designed three years after the war's end, Royère made dramatic use of very common materials—oak and goat fur—instead of a precious wood or expensive silk upholstery fabric.see p.44 While the humble materials signal the austerity of post-war France, a renewed interest in wood, rush, and other organic materials had already begun in the years before the war, as seen in the work of Charlotte Perriand following her visit to Japan. The use of goat fur imparts a sensuality to this work that is characteristic of French design, in general, and is especially evident in the work of pre-war decorators and furniture makers who used exotic woods, supple leathers, and fine textiles to achieve luxurious effects for wealthy clients. In the early 1950s, Jacques Adnet, an important tastemaker and the director of the Compagnie des arts français (an interior design and furnishings company established in 1919), invited Serge Mouille to design lighting fixtures for the company. Mouille's lighting fixtures bear the mark of French craft traditions. Trained as a silversmith, Mouille focused primarily on jewelry design and metal tableware. His carefully crafted and enameled pieces reveal his background as an artist/craftsman.

The impact of U.S. government intervention in France also had a marked influence on French production and, by extension, design. Recognizing the importance of cultural exchange with Europe to build political and cultural alliances, the U.S. government organized exhibitions and educational forums. Notably, the exhibition *Design for Use, USA* organized by the Museum of Modern Art, New York, in collaboration with the Department of State in

1952 (and presented at the Grand Palais in Paris), sought to build support in France for the American way of life. The exhibition showcased a wide range of American products, from washing machines and refrigerators to home furnishings, and was widely circulated in the press. It was at this time that examples of the innovative designs of Charles and Ray Eames and Eero Saarinen were brought to the attention of the French public. French designers responded in a variety of ways, as can be seen in the work of Pierre Paulin and Pierre Guariche, who experimented with new materials and techniques, such as plywood, aluminum, and fiberglass. Pierre Guariche's *Tonneau* chair in molded plywood (1954), produced by Steiner, was among the first commercially viable plywood chairs in France.[Fig.1] Guariche, Mathieu Mategot, Joseph-André Motte, and others, inspired by American examples, exploited the new materials and industrial techniques developed during wartime. New companies formed, such as Airborne and ARP (Atelier de recherche plastique), and established enterprises like Steiner and Roset redefined their production in response to the growing demand for home furnishings fueled by the post-war housing boom. In architecture, Le Corbusier's groundbreaking Unité d'habitation housing estate in Marseille (1947–1952) was developed using his "Modular" system of proportion. These high-density urban structures, radical in their approach to urban development and housing, expressed Le Corbusier's functional and technological approach to architecture and had a profound impact on urban planning in France and beyond. At the same time, the field of industrial design as a discipline distinct from the trades associated with interior design and decoration, flourished after the war in France. Professional organizations, trade fairs, and other outlets for the dissemination of industrial design took hold. In 1949, Formes utiles formed as an offshoot of the UAM. The organization promoted industrial design in France through exhibitions at the Salon des arts ménagers and through its magazine of the same name, read by designers, manufacturers, and retailers. In 1951, the Esthétique industrielle (Institute of Industrial Aesthetics) was organized by Jacques Viénot, and in 1956, the École national supérieure des arts appliqués (School of Applied Arts) introduced industrial aesthetics as a course of study.[1] In 1963, Roger Tallon established the Design Department of the École nationale supérieure des arts décoratifs in Paris. Reflecting on this years later, Tallon noted, "When I set up the Industrial Design section at the Decorative Arts school, I explained to the students that I was at the same point as them: I didn't know anything more, but I had a lot of practical experience."[2] Through his teaching, writing, and design work, which includes products such as the *Portavia PIII* portable television (1963); the *Cryptogamme* series commissioned by the Mobilier national for use in the cafeteria of the Grand Palais (1968) and later displayed at the French Pavilion at Expo '70 in Osaka, Japan; and the exterior and interiors of the Corail trains for the national railroad, Tallon remains one of the most important figures of French industrial design today.

France's national recovery was in full swing by the early 1960s, and industrial production was a key element. The American presence in France after the war—economically through the Marshall Plan, educationally through professional training offered in France and in the U.S., and culturally through American popular music, films, and advertising—had its supporters and detractors. Many in France, like President de Gaulle himself, were wary of the impact of America on French culture. In the face of increased Americanization, urbanization, and consumption, the French government

1. *Tonneau* chair, Pierre Guariche, 1954

22

took steps to preserve a uniquely French national identity. Education was one route. Since the end of the nineteenth century, France had mandated compulsory primary education, and in 1959 it was extended to the age of sixteen. The national education system bolstered the government's modernization and democratization project, and it instilled French language, culture, and civic responsibility into its young citizenry. In the same year, the government established the Ministry of Culture, under André Malraux, with the goal to "make accessible to the greatest number of French people the greatest works of humanity, beginning with those of France, to achieve the widest audience for our cultural heritage, and to promote the creation of works of art and the mind that will enrich it."[3]

The 1960s began with the uprising in Algeria to overthrow French domination and the continued civil war in the former colony of Vietnam, and then exploded with the student and work protests of May 1968. These events contributed to an atmosphere of unrest, disillusionment, and fear. French youth riots, while having specific reasons and associated outcomes for the French nation, also mirrored the protests in other large industrial nations such as the U.S. and Germany. Just twenty years after the conclusion of the Second World War, the unprecedented growth of an industrialized, consumer-based culture, in which ordinary objects became coveted and fetishized, prompted a backlash against industrialization and over commercialization. This implicit anti-Americanism was born out of the huge influx of American capital in France after the war and inflected by the current Cold War politics. Though a major commercial flop, Jacques Tati's dark comedy *Play Time* (1967) critiqued France's modernization project and Paris's new position as a playground for well-off American tourists.

The student and worker strikes of 1968 marked a turning point in French cultural politics. De Gaulle's top-down policies were seen as overly patriarchal and traditional, and increasingly out of step with youth culture. In response to student demands, the national university system added sixty-seven new universities and put in place a new system of governing councils. In the area of the arts, the government dismantled the studio and patron system at the École des beaux arts, France's elite art academy, and de-centralized arts education to form independent units in Paris and elsewhere.

Shortly after Georges Pompidou became president in 1969, he invited a group of designers and artists to design his private apartments at the Elysée Palace, the president's residence in Paris. Pierre Paulin designed a Bedouin-inspired smoking room with a tent-like structure, as well as a variety of seating pieces.see p.148 Pompidou also commissioned the Op artist Agam to create a three-dimensional installation for the drawing room, which included an extraordinary carpet woven at the centuries-old Gobelins manufactory.[4] The hierarchies between art and design dissolved, as they had done in earlier periods of history, and artists and designers worked alongside one another to create expressive environments and objects.

The Centre Beaubourg was conceived at the beginning of Pompidou's presidency in 1969 with the aim of bringing culture to the man on the street. Symbolically and physically demonstrating France's commitment to upholding and nurturing a democratic, national culture, the Centre's unconventional design by Renzo Piano and Richard Rogers literally turned the institution inside out. The fact that foreign architects were selected for the project reinforced France's status on the cutting edge of world culture. While intended for local audiences, this project (like the later Grand Louvre project by I. M. Pei) reaffirmed France's cultural leadership worldwide. With the intention to show all manifestations of contemporary art, the history of the Beaubourg's collection is closely linked with that of the Centre national des arts plastiques (National Center for Visual Arts, or CNAP). During this period, works were being purchased specifically for display at the new museum of modern art. [See Emilia Philippot's contribution to this catalogue.] That same year, the Centre de création industrielle (CCI) was organized to promote and document the nascent field of industrial design in France. Established as a part of the Union central des arts décoratifs (UCAD) at the Musée des arts décoratifs, the CCI later became a part of the Centre Georges Pompidou.

The reshaping of the relationship of the state to the public was also profoundly felt in the arena of urban housing. A backlash developed against the formalism proposed by Le Corbusier and the members of the Congrés internationaux d'architecture moderne (International Congress of Modern Architecture, or CIAM) after the war. By the late 1960s, Le Corbusier's slab and tower architecture came to be seen as inhuman.[5] In response, an expressionistic architecture replaced the functionalist model. Works such as Habitat 67 at Expo 67 in Montreal, for example, presented a new "polycubic" architecture.[6]

Striking new developments occurred during this time in the arena of home furnishings and industrial design, especially in small appliances and audio-visual devices. The popularity of unconventional, multi-functional, and collapsible or knockdown furnishings reveal changing mores that encouraged more informal social practices. Designers worked with new materials, primarily plastics, and used unconventional combinations of bright colors and patterns. Designers such as Pierre Paulin and Olivier Mourgue popularized organic, free form shapes.[Fig.2] Mourgue's *Djinn* chair (1965) was used in the science-fiction fantasy film *2001: A Space Odyssey* (1968) to embody the look of the future. Works by Marc Held such as the *Culbuto* armchair (1967), made of molded reinforced polyester fiberglass, utilized new techniques for forming plastic into continuous, structural shells.[Fig.3] Consumer demand also brought about changes in sales strategies. The Prisunic department store extended its reach to home furnishings in the mid-1960s, prompted by the success of Terence Conran's shops in London. In 1968, Prisunic launched a mail-order furniture catalog. The company produced and sold innovative and unconventional furnishings, working with designers such as Held, Danielle Quarante, Olivier Mourgue, and others.

Although it may seem like a folly today, in 1968 inflatable products were positioned as a provocative response to the social and political upheavals in France at that time. Members of the Utopie group, including architectural students Jean Aubert, Jean-Paul Jungmann, and Antoine Stinco, sociologists Hubert Tonka and Jean Baudrillard, and others proposed the restructuring of the relationship between everyday life, architecture, and urbanism. *Structures gonflables*, an exhibition at the Musée d'art moderne de la ville de Paris in 1968, brought together inflatable and pneumatic furnishings from a wide range of producers and presented three avant-garde projects that gave concrete form to a radical and utopian life built on air: Aubert's traveling theater; Jungmann's Dyodan house; and Stinco's traveling exhibition hall.[Fig.4] Architects and artists at the time viewed the inflatables as a "challenge to the weight, permanence, expense, and immobility of traditional architecture."[7] The aesthetic appeal of these avant-garde experiments resonated beyond the streets of the Latin Quarter. The French Pavilion at Expo' 70 in Osaka, Japan, for example, comprised a series of four geodesic, air-supported domes. Olivier Mourgue's anthropomorphic *Bouloum* chaise lounge, produced in foam covered metal, served as seating inside the pavilion, and outside the chaises served as fair "attendants," with some of them supporting signs that provided information or way finding.

2. *Dos à dos* bench,
Pierre Paulin, 1968

3. *Culbuto* armchair,
Marc Held, 1967

During Pompidou's presidency (1969–1974) an ambitious program of urban development and construction was completed, including several projects begun during De Gaulle's presidency. These included the development of La Défense, new transportation and public service facilities such as Orly airport, the Palais des Sports, and the Tour Montparnasse. When Giscard d'Estaing assumed the presidency (1974–1981), the economy was in recession and cultural spending declined slightly. Giscard's conservative policies focused more on the protection of cultural heritage than on new building projects. Two major redevelopment programs in Paris were initiated during his presidency: to turn the Gare d'Orsay into a museum of nineteenth century art, and to turn the abattoirs at La Villette into a museum of science.

In 1981, Socialist François Mitterrand was elected president of France. With the support of the National Assembly, Mitterrand initiated reforms that included nationalizing financial institutions and key industrial enterprises, raising the minimum wage, increasing social benefits, and abolishing the death penalty. Under Mitterrand's Minister of Culture, Jack Lang, the cultural agenda of the French Republic played a central role in the politics and economics of the state. During Mitterrand's presidency (1981–1995), the cornerstones of France's new cultural policy were developed, including the move toward the decentralization of culture to include areas outside of Paris, to foster great-

4. *Tore* ottoman,
A.J.S. Aerolande, 1967

er accessibility of cultural offerings to a wider public, and to encourage diversity and creativity in a wide variety of disciplines, from music to theater and the visual arts to architecture. Mitterrand understood that modernization, along with strengthening France's competitiveness with foreign powers such as the U.S. and Japan, were key factors in France's economic and political health. During Mitterrand's presidential campaign in 1980–1981, he outlined his political platform in "110 Propositions for France." In this document, Number 99 reads, "Support of the creative arts—cinematography, music, theater, plastic arts and architecture—will place cultural renaissance in France as one of the first major Socialist ambitions."[8] Mitterrand's *grand projets*, such as the expansion of the Musée du Louvre, the development of the Bibliothèque nationale, the establishment of the Institut du monde arabe, among others, were conceived with the intention of elevating France's cultural status by creating new public monuments for the capital of the Republic and reaffirming France's leadership status worldwide. Around this time the French launched a system to deliver networked information via the telephone system owned by the government. France Telecom distributed the device, called the Minitel, for free to households throughout France along with normal telephone service. The Minitel, from its inception, was viewed "as a tool of strategic social policy in France: a means…of promoting a particular vision of French social and political interaction."[9] A forerunner of the Internet, the Minitel allowed users to access telephone directories, book train tickets, and, as the system caught on and vendor participation increased, even to join online sex chat rooms.

A heightened awareness about design at this time prompted government-led initiatives to strengthen design education, production, and promotion. In the early 1980s, the New Design movement in Italy, later renamed Memphis, encouraged self-expression. Its re-evaluation of the role of the designer in industry had a profound effect on French design. At the Paris Furniture Fair in 1984, Edith Cresson, Minister of Industrial Reorganization and Foreign Trade, announced: "The Italian model is a model which ought to inspire us."[10] The Milanese Memphis group, established in late 1980, included two French designers, Martine Bedin and Natalie du Pasquier. Born and trained in France, both sought out opportunities in Italy, where designers and architects were questioning the relationship of the object to the consumer market. In the late 1970s Bedin worked at the radical architectural firm Superstudio in Florence, and du Pasquier, with her husband George Snowden, worked with Ettore Sottsass in Milan. Reinforcing the connection to Italy, works by Sottsass, Alessandro Mendini, and Andrea Branzi were among the early acquisitions of the CNAP.^{Fig. 5}

Recognizing the importance of bringing designers and industrialists together, the Ministry of Culture and the Ministry of Industry established the Valorisation de l'innovation en ameublement (Valorization of Innovation in Furnishing, or VIA) in 1980, and in 1982 created the École nationale supérieure de création industrielle (National School of Industrial Design or ENSCI; known today as Les Ateliers-Paris Design Institute) for the training of professionals to work with industry. When the CNAP was founded in 1982 to promote and support the arts in France, it included an acquisitions committee whose budget was devoted to decorative art, craft, and industrial design, to complement existing committees for the visual arts and photography.

The VIA aimed to strengthen and support French design in the furniture industry, with programs focused primarily on education, industry, and promotion. Among its initiatives were (and continue to be): the Carte Blanche award, a grant program to provide financial resources for design innovation; a prototype development initiative; and the promotion of French design through displays at trade fairs, such as the Milan Furniture Fair. In the 1980s VIA supported the work of Philippe Starck (Carte Blanche, 1982), who sketched fourteen new designs, including what would go into production as the *Don Denny* chair, used in the Café Costes; Martin Szekely (Carte Blanche, 1982), during which time he developed the *Pi* chaise lounge, a design he conceived of in carbon fiber, but realized in sheet metal;^{see p. 182} and Jean Nouvel (Carte Blanche, 1987), among others.

Philippe Starck is perhaps the most prolific designer to emerge from France during the 1980s. Like other students in the late 1960s in Paris, Starck took an irreverent, anti-establishment approach to his life and his work, designing inflatable structures—fragile and filled with air—during this period of social unrest. In 1969 he established his own firm and also worked as art director at Pierre Cardin, where he designed furniture. By 1983, he was propelled into the national headlines with his designs for the private apartments of President Mitterrand at the Elysée Palace. One critic noted that Starck "demonstrated his incredible aptitude for dismantling 'bourgeois' taste and exposing its banality."[11] This assessment rests, in part, on Starck's design for a club chair that would eventually go into production as *Richard III*.^{see p. 64} Seen from the front, the chair resembles a typical side chair with a wide frame, overstuffed cushions, and leather upholstery; seen from the back, its entire steel frame is exposed. Starck would go on to forge an international career of mega-proportion with building and interior design projects such as the Café Costes in Paris, the Asahi Beer Hall in Tokyo, and the Royalton Hotel in New York City; and an A to Z of products for companies worldwide, including France's XO, Decaux, and Louis Vuitton; Germany's Duravit; and Italy's Alessi, Cassina, Driade, and Kartell, among others.

During the 1980s, other French designers grabbed headlines. Galerie Neotu, which opened in Paris in 1984 (and in New York City

5. *Carlton* library,
Ettore Sottsass, 1980

in 1990), promoted the work of young, French designers and contributed to the successful careers of Elizabeth Garouste and Mattia Bonetti, François Bauchet, Olivier Gagnère, and many others. Claiming the title "new barbarians," Garouste and Bonetti (also awarded a Carte Blanche in 1989) set aside established notions of formality, hierarchy, and even civility in their work and re-positioned traditional materials, such as bronze, leather, gilded metal, and wood, within an avant-garde narrative that poked fun at bourgeois values. Bonetti continues his experimentation with materials and forms to express psycho-social relationships and meanings, as demonstrated by the *Armoire mur* (2006).

By the mid-1990s, Starck had mentored an entire generation of designers, including matali crasset, Patrick Jouin, and Jean-Marie Massaud. From 1992 to 1997 Starck served as creative director of Tim Thom, a division of the French-owned electronics firm, Thomson. Working with many of his protégés, Starck conceived of the so-called "dream products" that served a communication function, beyond their functional one: the *Alo* telephone, the *Icipari* radio, and the *Rock 'n' Rock* stereo system, to name just a few, played with preconceived ideas about meaning and function.

Many French designers emerged on the international scene in the 1990s, a result, in part, of the government's investment in the 1980s in design education and dissemination. It is not surprising to learn that many of today's celebrated French designers were supported by VIA. Among the recipients of the Carte Blanche award in the 1990s and the early 2000s were: Pierre Charpin (1995), Patrick Jouin (1997), Frédéric Ruyant (2002), and François Azambourg (2005).[Fig. 6, 7, 8]

The approach of the new millennium was the catalyst for Starck's very personal line of "non-products" for La Redoute mail order catalogue, called the *Good Goods*. *Good Goods* took an optimistic approach to the millennium in its suggestion that design with good intentions could elevate man's existence by solving real problems. While technocrats worried that the Y2K bug would wipe out computer networks, no one anticipated the tragic events of September 11, 2001, or its aftermath: the "war on terror," heightened security risks, and sharp economic decline.

7. *Mobilier en ligne / Ligne de mobilier*, Frédéric Ruyant, 1999

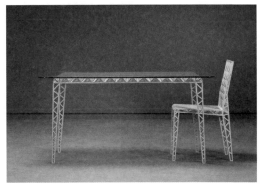

8. *Very Nice* table and chair, François Azambourg, 2004

6. *Solid C2* chair, Patrick Jouin, 2004

Designers turned away from design as a commodity, choosing instead to solve functional problems through the application of new digital technologies, such as rapid prototyping. François Brument experimented with recorded sound to develop a digital design program to create the *Vase #44* project through rapid prototyping.see p. 186 Designer Mathieu Lahanneur tackled the complex relationship between patients and the delivery of medications. Other designers looked to traditional processes, participating in government-sponsored programs to bolster craft production, such as those offered at Sèvres, CIRVA (Centre international de recherche sur le verre) in Marseille, and Vallauris; still others addressed diminished economic resources and increased environmental issues with suggestions to "mend" or "make do" with existing resources, such as 5.5's *Prothèse d'assise* (2004–6).[Fig. 9] For designer matali crasset, life's everyday situations offer opportunities to apply her creativity, common sense, and perhaps even sense of humor. Works such as *Quand Jim Monte à Paris* (1995) and the *Digestion* series (2000) resolve real-life conditions faced by those living in small places.

Today, designers in France embody in their work a multitude of approaches. Some embrace highly technical means of production, while others challenge social constructs to reshape our engagement with the world. The global market, instantaneous access to information, and new production technologies, like rapid prototyping, have already shattered the boundaries of time and space. Design practice is informed by personal engagement with the world, and the view from France is rich, multifaceted, and evolving.

9. *Le robot porte fruits ou légumes,*
Florence Doléac, 2001

—
Notes

1. In 1949, Viénot established one of the first industrial design firms in France, Technès, and in 1953 hired Roger Tallon as the technical and artistic director. He also taught the first graduate course in industrial design at the École des arts appliques à l'industrie.
2. Gilles de Bure and Chloé Braunstein, *Roger Tallon* (Paris: Editions Dis Voir, 1999), 54.
3. Malraux, circular of 3 February 1959, quoted by Robert Gildea, *France Since 1945* (London: Oxford University Press, 2002), 200.
4. The Agam room is on display at the Centre Georges Pompidou, Paris.
5. Joseph Abram, "Political Will and the Cultural Identity Crisis in Late-Twentieth-Century French Architecture", in *Premises. Invested Spaces in Visual Arts, Architecture, and Design from France: 1958–1998* (New York: Guggenheim Museum and Harry N. Abrams, 1999), 334–355.
6. Ibid, 338.
7. Marc Dessauce, *The Inflatable Moment: Pneumatics and Protest in '68* (New York: Architectural League of New York), 8.
8. Denis MacShane, *Francois Mitterrand, a Political Odyssey* (New York: Universe Books, 1982), 271.
9. Jack Kessler, "The French Minitel. Is There Digital Life Outside of the 'US ASCII' Internet? A Challenge or a Convergence," *D-LIB Magazine*, December 1995. http://www.dlib.org/dlib/december95/12kessler.html.
10. Odile Rousseau, "L'appel de Milan/Appeal of Milan," in *VIA Design 3.0* (Paris: Centre Pompidou and Valorixation de l'innovation dans l'ameublement, 2009), 78.
11. *L'Art de Vivre, Decorative Arts and Design in France, 1789–1989* (New York: Vendome Press and Cooper-Hewitt Museum, 1989), 251.

—

Figure list

Fig. 1. *Tonneau* chair, 1954
Pierre Guariche [French, 1926–1995]
Société Steiner [France], producer
Moulded plywood, black lacquered iron, cloth
30 ⅜ × 19 ⅝ × 15 ⅜"
77 × 50 × 39 cm

Fig. 2. *Dos à dos* bench, 1968
Pierre Paulin [French, 1927–2009]
Mobilier national et Manufactures
des Gobelins, de Beauvais et de la
Savonnerie [France], manufacturer
White painted metal, foam polyester, jersey
24 ⅜ × 68 ½ × 23 ⅝"
62 × 174 × 60 cm

Fig. 3. *Culbuto* armchair, 1967
Marc Held [French, *1932]
Knoll Associates [USA], producer, 1970
Reinforced polyester fiberglass hull,
fabric covered foam-lined cast
47 ¼ × 34 ¼ × 29 ⅜"
120 × 87 × 74.5 cm

Fig. 4. *Tore* ottoman, 1967
A.J.S. Aerolande [French, est. 1960s]
Jean Aubert [French, *1935];
Jean-Paul Jungmann [French, *1935];
Antoine Stinco [Tunisian, *1934]
Piermag, producer
Polyvinyl chloride, fabric
13 ¾ × ø 21 ⅝"
35 × ø 55 cm

Fig. 5. *Carlton* library, 1980
Ettore Sottsass [Italian, b. Austria, 1917–2007]
Memphis s.r.l. [Italy], producer
Wood veneer laminated plastic
77 ⅛ × 74 ¾ × 15 ¾"
196 × 190 × 40 cm

Fig. 6. *Solid C2* chair, prototype, 2004
Patrick Jouin [French, *1967]
Materiralise MGX [Belgium], manufacturer
30 ¾ × 16 ⅛ × 20 ½ in
78 × 41 × 52 cm

Fig. 7. *Mobilier en ligne /
Ligne de mobilier*, 1999
Frédéric Ruyant [French, *1961]
Ministère de la Culture et de la
communication, commissioner through
"Fiacre" research grantwork
MDF (Medium-density fiberboard)
71 ⅝ × 186 ¼ × 35 ⅜"
182 × 473 × 90 cm

Fig. 8. *Very Nice* table and chair, 2004
François Azambourg [French, *1963]
Domeau & Pérès [France],
producer, 2005–2010
Structure and frame natural
Birch ply, shelf glass
28 × 50 ⅜ × 30"
71 × 128 × 76 cm

Fig. 9. *Le robot porte fruits ou légumes*, 2001
Florence Doléac [French, *1968]
Atelier La Poterie d'Amélie
[France], manufacturer, and Radi
Designers [France], producer
Glazed earthenware
18 ⅜ × ø 14 ¾ "
46.5 × ø 37.5 cm

THE CENTRE NATIONAL
DES ARTS PLASTIQUES
COLLECTION OF DECORATIVE ARTS, CRAFT,
AND DESIGN: A FRENCH EXCEPTION
Emilia Philippot

The Centre national des arts plastiques (National Center for Visual Arts, or CNAP) is located in the business district of La Défense, just outside central Paris. Established in 1982, the CNAP oversees the largest collection of international art in France, comprising more than ninety thousand pieces of art, organized in three main categories: visual arts; photography; and decorative arts, craft, and industrial design. The origin of the collection stretches back to the end of the eighteenth century, at which time the government set aside funds for the acquisition of works of art for the national patrimony, independent of museums. The unique identity of the collection has been shaped mostly by administrative changes (or evolutions) in the French government towards its cultural policy. Truly an exceptional feature of the national art scene in France, the history of the CNAP exemplifies the complex relationship that the State, in its role as art collector, maintains with artistic creativity.[1] This essay provides a brief overview of the CNAP's history, focusing primarily on the collection of decorative arts, craft, and industrial design from which the exhibition, *Liberty, Equality, and Fraternity* is drawn.

ONCE UPON A TIME

The collection of the CNAP traces its history back to 1791, just after the French Revolution, when the new government established a budgetary line for the acquisition of art works to be exhibited or shown in places such as museums, ministries, embassies, courthouses, hospitals, universities, prefectures, and military buildings. This act of state cultural sponsorship aimed to achieve two objectives, perhaps paradoxical. The first goal was to encourage awareness of and interest in emerging artists by displaying their work; in that regard, it was a prospective mission with the aim of creating future collections. The second goal was to provide financial assistance to the most destitute artists as an expression of the social and democratic vision of the newly formed government. As a result, the State's earliest acquisitions represent a wide range of styles and levels of quality. By 1875, an advisory council made up of artists and art critics called the Conseil supérieur des beaux-arts (Supreme Council of Fine Arts) was put in place to participate in the selection of works for the State collection. French

cultural policy towards the acquisition of new works of art remained relatively unchanged until 1961, when a genuinely new and open policy towards contemporary art was set forth by Minister of Cultural Affairs André Malraux. In his view, "the business of the State is not to supervise art, but to serve it." Malraux, who was appointed during the presidency of Charles De Gaulle, established the cultural agenda of the State with a focus on three key areas: the promotion and protection of French cultural heritage, or patrimony; the cultivation of creativity and cultural production; and the dissemination of culture to a wide audience in France, and abroad. These principles continue to inform French cultural policy today.

The program to create a national museum of modern art, which took shape under the leadership of President Georges Pompidou, reinvigorated the State's contemporary art acquisition policy. Between 1969 and 1976, the State focused its funding on building the collection of the future Musée national d'art moderne (National Museum of Modern Art, or MNAM), purchasing representative works of contemporary art for display. With the contemporary collections growing and in anticipation of the opening of the MNAM (renamed the Centre Georges Pompidou), in 1976 the government established the Fonds national d'art contemporain (National Contemporary Art Fund, or FNAC) to oversee and continue its program of supporting the work of living artists to be shown at the MNAM. Charged with the oversight of the entire State art collection, the FNAC pursued a deaccessioning program, keeping only art works considered likely to be loaned for exhibition or to be donated to another museum. Collection objects intended for use or display in official government buildings were assigned to the Mobilier national, a national agency overseeing all furniture and art for ministerial residencies and other agencies. A major turning point regarding the history of the State art collection occurred in 1981, with the election of François Mitterrand as France's socialist president. Mitterrand proposed a new cultural policy, which some observers likened to the New Deal art programs established in the United States in the 1930s. Under the leadership of Minister of Culture Jack Lang, an unprecedented increase in the cultural budget occurred, and the Délégation aux arts plastiques (Delegation of Visual Arts) was established to support and promote contemporary creation in all visual arts disciplines under the auspices of the newly created CNAP in 1982.[2] The CNAP was founded to serve a dual purpose: to oversee all the works in the inventory of the FNAC and to continue the government's policy of collecting new works of French and international art.

Art works from the collection continued to be loaned to government offices, embassies, and ministries, and increasingly to museums outside of the Parisian environs.[3] In keeping with Mitterrand's policy of cultural decentralization, the CNAP launched a regionalization plan to help museums develop their own contemporary art collections. At that time, the purchasing policy guidelines were extensively modified, and acquisitions were driven by partnerships with other cultural institutions. The Ministry of Culture and Communication established regional cultural centers and funding associations financed mutually by the State and the regions. This new geographical breadth led to a repositioning of the State's art acquisition policy as well as to an overhaul of the system.

THE STATE AS ART COLLECTOR:
USER'S MANUAL
In 1982, the CNAP established three commissions to guide acquisitions, each corresponding to a readily defined aspect of the collection: visual arts; photography; and decorative arts, craft, and industrial design. The commissions are appointed by the Ministry of Culture and Communication and are composed of qualified people such as designers, art critics, art collectors, historians, and ex-officio representatives of national cultural agencies, such as the Ministry of Culture, Musée des arts décoratifs, and the Sèvres porcelain manufactory, among others. Commission members serve a non-renewable term of three years, on a voluntary basis.[4] Their varied backgrounds and experiences allows for a plurality of perspectives about the collection and contributes to the diversity of work acquired. Over the past twenty years, commission members have included designers Mattia Bonetti, Raymond Guidot, Renny Ramakers (co-founder of Droog Design),

and Philippe Starck; Alexander Vegesack, director of the Vitra Museum; and Valérie Guillaume, curator of design, Centre Georges Pompidou. Each member is encouraged to share their personal philosophy regarding the composition of the collection and the role it plays in the advancement of the national patrimony. Dominique Bozo, former director of the Musée Picasso and the MNAM, noted the limits of this system: "A committee is only as good as the ambitions or motivations that inspire it, before being worth the quality of its members or the importance of its means."[5] By the early 1990s, the various committees were defining the guiding principles of a concerted, coherent, and clearly stated acquisition policy. According to this newly defined perspective, support for young designers and relationships with other public collections were ongoing priorities to be regularly reinforced by the various government institutions supporting cultural policies.

Several key principles guide the acquisition committee. Members of the committee meet two to three times a year. They are responsible for reviewing individual applications from artists or galleries that present their portfolios directly to the CNAP; for presenting purchase proposals; and for putting the sellers in contact with the CNAP's acquisition office. When committees are in session all potential acquisitions are presented to the members, and then a vote is taken by secret ballot using a rating system. The works that have obtained the highest scores are kept until the budget is exhausted.[6] In the event of a tie vote, the committee chairman's vote prevails. All discussions are confidential and abstention from voting is required in cases where a committee member has a personal or professional relationship with an artist whose work is being considered for purchase.

At the conclusion of the committee's negotiations (including discussions about the cost of works), the purchase proposals are submitted to the Minister of Culture. If agreement is reached on an acquisition, the work is purchased and it becomes part of the collection. New works are then inventoried, registered, and documented. Catalogue information and a digital image is entered into a database system accessible on Videomuseum (see videomuseum.fr) and the works become available for short- and long-term loans.

DESIGN AS "STOCK": MULTIPLE POINTS OF VIEW

The collection of decorative arts, craft, and industrial design fits readily into the political context of the 1980s in which many other initiatives supporting industrial design were established, such as the Agence pour la promotion de la création industrielle (Agency for the Promotion of Industrial Design, or APCI), whose aim is to foster cooperation between designers and manufacturers through competitions and exhibitions, and the École nationale supérieure de création industrielle (National School for Creation of Industrial Design), which trains the designers of the future. President Mitterrand's *grands projets*, also conceived at this time, relied heavily on designers; design commissions awarded included Gae Aulenti for the interior of the Musée d'Orsay, Philippe Starck for furniture for the Parc de la Villette, and Jean-Michel Wilmotte for the reception and circulation areas of the Grand Louvre.

While reflecting the growing interest of the public authorities for the applied arts, the purchases made by the CNAP, unlike those made by museums in the same period, do not fit a well-defined policy of enrichment.[7] The first assessment of the collection, published in *Acquisition arts décoratifs 1982–1990*, lists some 1,200 pieces of decorative art registered with the CNAP. Objects are divided into three distinct categories: design (furniture, lighting, and patented objects), textiles (objects made according to the principles of weaving), and glass [primarily works made at the Centre international de la recherche sur le verre et les arts plastiques (International Center for Research on Glass and Visual Arts, or CIRVA)].[8] The guiding principles of the acquisition policy are limited to two objectives: to meet the demand of regional museums and to respond positively to the output of young artists working with traditional materials or adopting traditional techniques. The outlook for the future is based on two major objectives: a greater openness towards the industrialized object and an increasing number of long-term loans in museums. This policy is reflected by the focus on monographic collections dedicated to significant contemporary artists.

Due to the CNAP's regular program of purchases, the collection now exceeds 6,500 pieces created by more than 1,530 artists (craftsmen, designers, architects, and visual artists), and it comprises furniture, lighting fixtures, tabletop pieces, textiles, and also, more moderately, jewelry, household appliances, audio-visual equipment, and fashion. Among the notable works in the collection are those by Italian designers Ettore Sottsass, Alessandro Mendini, Gaetano Pesce, and Andrea Branzi; French designers Martin Szekely, Olivier Gagnère, Philippe Starck, Elizabeth Garouste and Mattia Bonetti; and Dutch designers Jurgen Bey, Hella Jungerius, and Marcel Wanders. The CNAP also invests in the work of emerging designers, and as a result has early works by the likes of Ronan and Erwan Bouroullec, Radi Designers, matali crasset, 5.5, Delo Lindo, and Pierre Charpin. Owing to its broad focus, the CNAP collection provides a snapshot of decorative arts, craft, and industrial design of the last thirty years, observing the changes in relationships that have developed over time among the creators, publishers, manufacturers, and distributors of design.

The value, originality, and significance of this unique collection lies in the multitude of perspectives it encompasses. This multifaceted approach is evident in the operation of the committee that calls for a dynamic interaction between a variety of points of view and experiences. It is also reflected in the title of the collection: "Decorative arts, craft, and industrial design," which, as was demonstrated in the outstanding exhibition *Design en stock* (Design in Stock), does not impose a single system of classification on the various components of the collection. Instead, the collection is considered as a whole, and the CNAP invites those who use it to apply their own order.[9] Christine Colin, inspector of artistic creation in charge of design at the Ministry of Culture and Communication, and curator of Design in Stock, proposed a reading of the collection through thirteen filters, including national origin, production method, materials, or dimensions, among others. The CNAP also aims to represent all stages of an object's life cycle: from the sketch to the prototype, from the unique piece to a reissue or reproduction. Whereas museums generally seek to acquire original editions, the CNAP documents the various stages of a design's existence. Objects that are foldable, stackable, or collapsible are always purchased in multiples in order to display their various configurations simultaneously. As a consequence, the CNAP collects a great number of works; more, in fact, than any other French cultural institution dedicated to design.

In sum, it is "openness" that characterizes the decorative arts collection of the CNAP. "The approach of the FNAC," as Christine Colin observed, "is closer to the spirit of the inventory of artistic resources launched by Minister of Culture André Malraux in 1964 than to a collection built from an historical perspective. In the spirit of André Malraux, the inventory should be a tool to expand our field of vision."[10] Whether it is made available to museums for long-term loan, or accessible online through the Design Portal (see portaildesign. fr), or presented at exhibitions in France and abroad, the non-specialized or general nature of the collection offers a wide variety of materials from which various partners are invited to draw from and to develop their own discourse on artistic activity.[11]

—
Notes

1. The value of a museum's collection owes much to its degree of specialization, or at least its overall consistency (curators seek to fill gaps and build connections).
2. In 1982, Jack Lang secured an increase of 101.3 percent for its culture budget, which was extended by a further increase of 17 percent in 1983. Over the course of those two years, the allocation for culture in the State budget increased from 0.48 percent to 0.74 percent. See Emmanuel Waresquiel, ed., *Dictionnaire des politiques culturelles de la France depuis 1959* (Paris: Larousse / CNRS Editions, 2001), 672.
3. The "depot", or long-term loan, is an important tool for the dissemination of the collections to public institutions throughout France. In 1998, for example, more than a hundred works were put on loan at the newly opened Musée d'art moderne de Strasbourg.
4. Article 14 of the ruling procedure of the Advisory Committee responsible for the acquisition of works of art: Decree No. 82-883 of October 15, 1982 concerning the establishment of the CNAP, and amended by Decree No. 2007-1758 of December 13, 2007.
5. Report on the Acquisition Committee established by the Survey of Artistic Creation, 1987, quoted by Ann Hindry, "Le FNAC, une si longue histoire," *Art contemporain* (Paris: Editions du Chêne, 2001), 33.
6. An average score of at least 10/20 is required.
7. Such is the case, for instance, with the Musée des arts décoratifs and the Centre de création industrielle (CCI).
8. For reasons of space, the ceramics were treated separately.
9. *Design en stock*, Palais de la Porte Dorée, Paris, October 20, 2004–January 16, 2005.
10. See Christine Colin, "Design en stock," in *Question(s) design* (Paris: Flammarion, 2010), 286.
11. Supported by a national digitization program of the Ministry of Culture and Communication, portaildesign.fr is an online database devoted exclusively to objects and furniture of the twentieth and twenty-first centuries in the collections of four major public institutions: Les Arts décoratifs, the CNAP, the Centre Pompidou, and the Musée d'art moderne de Saint-Etienne Métropole.

The design objects presented here are organized as a series of nine narrative clusters conceived in the French literary tradition of depicting peculiar personae. Each cluster considers an important theme, personality, or context. Collectively, they comprise a reading of French design history from the 1940s to today that illustrates the capacity of design to operate as a politically relevant aesthetic practice.

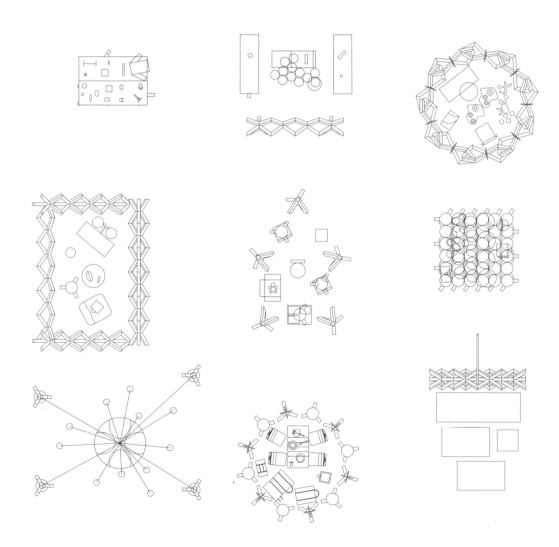

A Jean Royère armchair, an Hermès
Kelly handbag, and a ceramic baguette
disclose aesthetic and political
narratives that are central to this
project. Together they delineate a
new framework for evaluating French
design history and examining some
of its basic assumptions.

Armchair, 1948
Jean Royère [French, 1902–1981]
Oak chair with cylindrical armrests,
goat fur
31 $\frac{7}{8}$ × 33 $\frac{1}{2}$ × 41 $\frac{1}{4}$"
81 × 85 × 105 cm

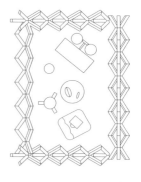

Kelly handbag, 1935
Hermès International [Paris],
manufacturer, 2008
Smooth full grain leather,
chrome tanning, gold-plated clasp,
four circular metal goldplated pads
14 $^1/_4$ × 12 $^7/_8$ × 4 $^3/_4$"
36 × 32.5 × 12 cm

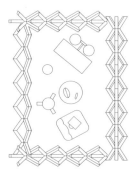

Petit Pain box, 1978
Pierre Baey [French, *1940]
Artist's edition
Earthenware
2 $^{3}/_{8}$ × 5 $^{7}/_{8}$ × 3"
6 × 15 × 7.5 cm

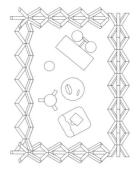

Saturne lamp, 1958
Serge Mouille [French, 1922–1988]
Artist's edition
Brass, spun aluminum
12 $^3/_8$ × ø 13"
31.5 × ø 33 cm

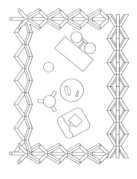

School desk PP 11,
from the School furniture series,
1935
Ateliers Jean Prouvé [France],
1946–1952, manufacturer
Wood, metal
Table: 44 $^7/_8$ × 18 $^1/_8$ × 28 $^1/_4$"
114 × 46 × 72 cm
Chairs: 28 × 13 $^5/_8$"
71 × 34.5 cm

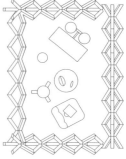

THE SYSTEM

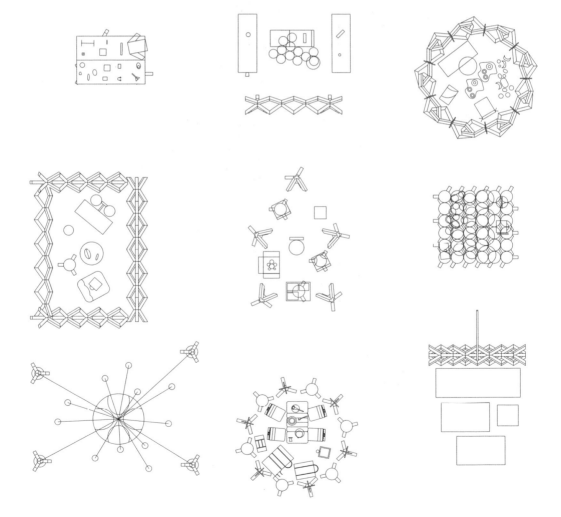

The work produced by "star" designer
Philippe Starck joins two traditions
of French design often described
as contradictory poles: anonymous,
industrial design for the many, and
expressive design for an elite clientele.
In Starck's practice, the voice of the
designer speaks through the object,
challenging the silence of standardized
product design.

Jim Nature portable television,
model, 1993
Philippe Starck [French, *1949]
for Tim Thom
Thomson, Saba [France], manufacturer
Plastic, high-density wood,
glass screen
14 $^5/_8$ × 15 $^3/_8$ × 15"
37 × 39 × 38 cm

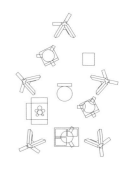

La Maison de Ph. Starck kit, 1994
Philippe Starck [French, *1949]
Trois Suisses [France], producer
Wood, paper, mixed media
3 $^7/_8$ × 31 $^7/_8$ × 24 $^3/_4$"
8.5 × 79.6 × 62.5 cm

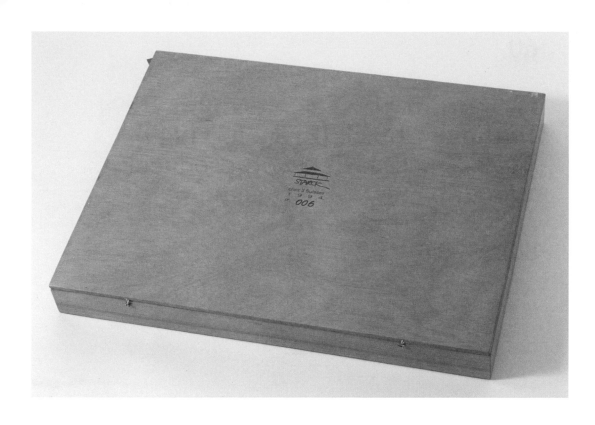

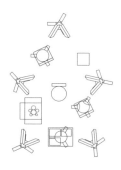

Oz portable television, 1993
Philippe Starck [French, *1949]
for Tim Thom
Thomson, Telefunken [France],
manufacturer
Plastic, mahogany veneer, nickel,
glass screen
14 × 14 $^5/_8$ × 14 $^1/_4$"
35.6 × 37 × 36.3 cm

Richard III armchair, 1984
Philippe Starck [French, *1949]
Baleri [Italy], producer
Rigid polyurethane painted metallic
silver, cushions in polyurethane foam
and Dacron covered with black cloth
35 $\frac{1}{2}$ × 36 $\frac{3}{8}$ × 31 $\frac{1}{2}$"
91 × 92.5 × 80 cm

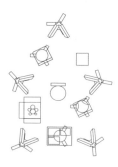

TeddyBearBand toy, 1998
Philippe Starck [French, *1949]
La Redoute [France], producer
Moulin Roty [France], manufacturer
Cotton
13 $^3/_4$ × 14 $^1/_4$ × 10 $^1/_4$"
35 × 36 × 26 cm

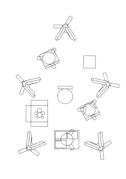

Le théâtre du monde desk, 1985
Philippe Starck [French, *1949]
Trois Suisses [France], producer
Steel sheet powder coated in black
44 $^7/_8$ × 13 $^3/_8$ × 16 $^1/_8$"
114 × 39 × 41 cm

Toilet, 1994
Philippe Starck [French, *1949]
Duravit AG [Germany], manufacturer
Ceramic
40 $^5/_8$ × 24 $^3/_4$ × 16 $^1/_8$"
103 × 63 × 41 cm

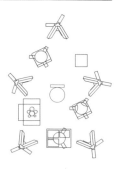

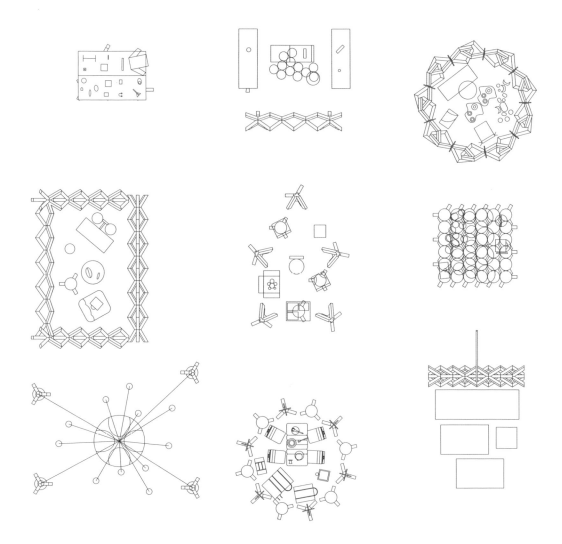

In the 1990s, Tim Thom, the research and development department of the French electronics firm Thomson, introduced a groundbreaking program in which designers gave form to a collection of Dream Products. These physical embodiments of technological desire reintroduced human eccentricity and atavism into the depersonalized sphere of consumer electronics.

Alo telephone, model, 1995
Philippe Starck [French, *1949],
concept and artistic direction,
and Jérôme Olivet [French, *1971],
design, for Tim Thom
Dream Products collection
Thomson [France], manufacturer
Cast aluminum embedded in resin,
varnish and transfer print, aluminum,
marble base
Phone: 12 × 19 $^3/_4$ × 15"
30.5 × 50 × 38 cm
Pipette: 3 $^7/_8$ × ø 1 $^3/_8$"
10 × ø 3.5 cm
Base: $^3/_4$ × 19 $^3/_4$ × 15"
2.1 × 50 × 38 cm

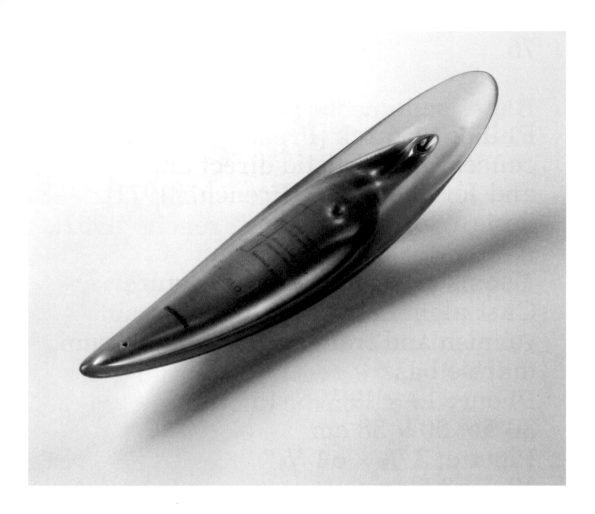

Babel multimedia projector,
model, 1995
Philippe Starck [French, *1949],
concept and artistic direction,
and Gérard Vergneau [French, *1952],
design, for Tim Thom
Dream Products collection
Thomson [France], manufacturer
Painted laminated polyester shell,
painted plastic feet, plastic and glass
lens, painted plastic enclosure
66 $^7/_8$ × 8 $^1/_4$ × 22"
170 × 21 × 56 cm

Boa portable radio, model, 1995
Philippe Starck [French, *1949],
concept and artistic direction,
and Claude Bressan [Italian, *1943],
design, for Tim Thom
Dream Products collection
Thomson, Saba [France], manufacturer
Leather, saddle stitching, iron etching,
painted brass
1 1/4 × 3 3/4 × 3 1/2"
3 × 9.6 × 9 cm

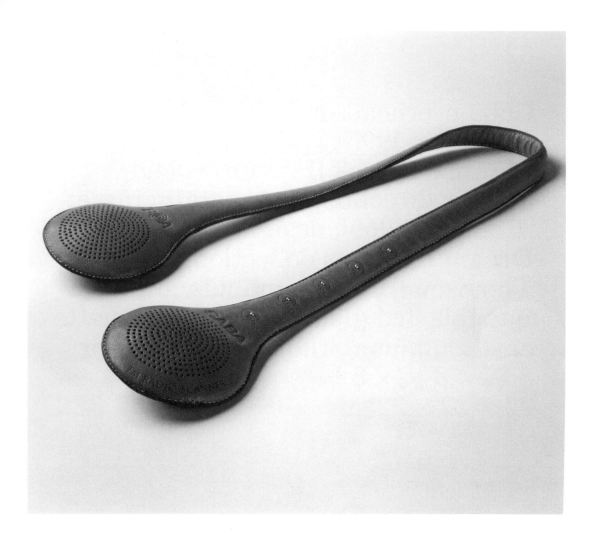

Cube overhead projector – LCD
projector, 1995
Philippe Starck [French, *1949],
artistic direction, and matali crasset
[French, *1965], design, for Tim Thom
Dream Products collection
Thomson [France], manufacturer
Sandblasted glass screen, semi-matte
cast aluminum, rubber rope, mirror
8 $^3/_4$ × 8 $^3/_4$ × 8 $^3/_4$"
22 × 22 × 22 cm

Krazy Jacket personal stereo,
prototype, 1995
Philippe Starck [French, *1949],
artistic direction, Patrick Jouin [French,
*1967], concept, and Michael Michalsky
[German, *1967], design, for Tim Thom
Dream Products collection
Thomson, Saba [France] and Adidas
[Germany], manufacturers
Nylon jacket, Walkman, speakers,
amplifier
31 ¹/₂ × 59 ¹/₈"
80 × 150 cm

Hollow Voices 1 radio, model, 1999
Laurent Massaloux [French, *1968]
for Tim Thom
Thomson [France], manufacturer
Wood, perforated metal, Plexiglas
2 ³/₈ × 5 ³/₄ × 3 ¹/₂"
6 × 14.5 × 9 cm

Hollow Voices 2 [Memo]
voice recorder, model, 1999
Olivier Sidet [French, *1965]
and Laurent Massaloux
[French, *1968], for Tim Thom
Thomson [France], manufacturer
Plastic
3 ½ × ø3"
9 × ø7.5 cm

LaLaLa radio, 1994
Philippe Starck [French, *1949]
for Tim Thom
Thomson [France], manufacturer
Bakelite, FM wire antenna, metal
speaker grill
11 × ø7 $^{7}/_{8}$"
28 × ø20 cm

Moa Moa radio, 1994
Philippe Starck [French, *1949]
for Tim Thom
Thomson [France], manufacturer
Bakelite, LCD, FM wire antenna
wrapped in plastic, metal speaker grill
4 ¼ × 9 ⅛ × 5 ½"
11 × 23 × 14 cm

Moosk radio, 1996
Jérôme Olivet [French, *1971]
for Tim Thom
Thomson [France] and Alessi [Italy],
manufacturers
Polypropylene
3 1/8 × 8 1/4 × 5 1/8"
8 × 21 × 13 cm

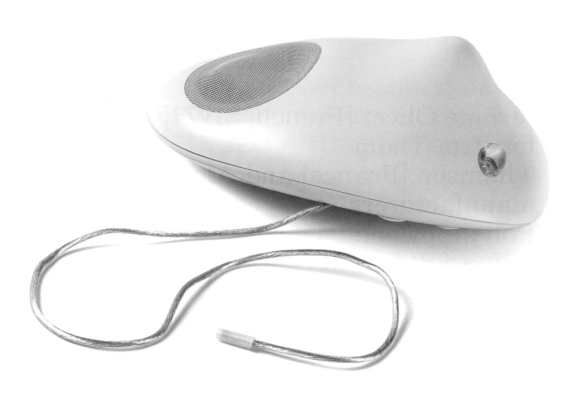

Perso portable videophone
in a leather case, model, 1995
Philippe Starck [French, *1949],
concept and artistic direction,
and matali crasset [French, *1965],
design, for Tim Thom
Dream Products collection
Thomson, Telefunken [France],
manufacturer
Hermès leather, Plexiglas, paint,
varnish, transfer print
45 $^3/_4$ × 57 $^1/_8$ × 4 $^1/_4$"
116 × 145 × 11 cm

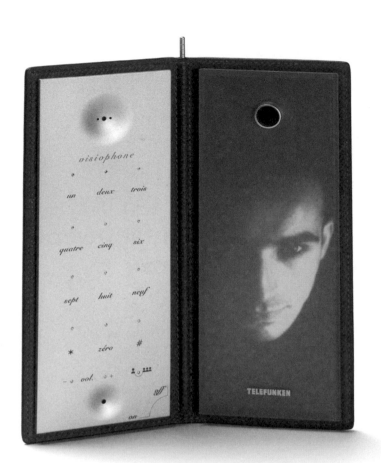

Porcelaine radio, prototype, 1999
Elsa Frances [French, *1966]
for Tim Thom
Thomson [France] and Centre
de recherche sur les arts du feu
et de la terre [France], manufacturers
Porcelain, polyurethane foam
4 1/4 × ø 7 1/2"
11 × ø 19 cm

THOMSON

Rock 'n' Rock stereo system,
model, 1995
Philippe Starck [French, *1949],
concept and artistic direction, and
Elsa Frances [French, *1966], design,
for Tim Thom
Dream Products collection
Thomson, Telefunken [France],
manufacturer
Polyurethane resin, metal,
polyurethane paint, transfer print,
acrylic, varnish
Radio: $3/4$ × 7 $1/8$ × 7 $1/8$"
1.7 × 18 × 18 cm
Personal stereo: 2 × 5 $1/2$ × 5 $1/8$"
5 × 14 × 13 cm
Speaker: 3 × 4 $1/4$ × 5 $1/8$"
7.5 × 11 × 13 cm
Speaker: 2 $3/4$ × 3 $7/8$ × 4 $3/4$"
7 × 10 × 12 cm

TELEFUNKEN rock°rock

Street Master radio, model, 1995
Philippe Starck [French, *1949],
concept, Claude Bressan [Italian, *1943],
design, for Tim Thom
Thomson, Saba [France], manufacturer
Painted carbon steel, painted
polystyrene keys
68 ¹/₂ × ø3 ¹/₄"
174 × ø 8.2 cm

Toccata CD player, model, 1995
Philippe Starck [French, *1949],
artistic direction, and Manuela
Simonelli [Italian, *1971] and
Andrea Quaglio [Italian, *1965],
design, for Tim Thom
Dream Products collection
Thomson [France], manufacturer
Cherry wood, Plexiglass, polyurethane
resin, paint, varnish, transfers
11 ³/₄ × 15 ³/₄ × 2"
30 × 40 × 5 cm

Vertigo video projector, prototype, 1995
Philippe Starck [French, *1949],
artistic direction, and Jean-Michel
Policar [French, *1970], design,
for Tim Thom
Dream Products collection
Thomson, Saba [France], manufacturer
Aluminum, bronze, plexiglas screen
21 ³/₄ × 8 ¹/₄ × 16 ¹/₈"
55 × 21 × 41 cm

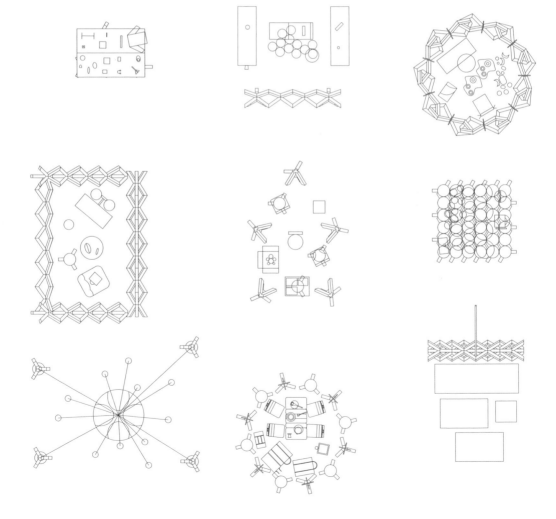

For centuries, French design
has been linked to political culture.
Grounded in reason and regulation,
the administrative ethos of the modern
French state has been critiqued as
prohibiting individual expression,
with all of its excess and sensuality.
The efficient elegance of the Bouroullec
Brothers' La Valise is a formal
reminder of this intensely rational
spirit.

Carafe, 1999
Ronan Bouroullec [French, *1971]
Torique collection
Des designers à Vallauris,
Ministère de la Culture et de la
Communication, commissioner
Galerie Gilles Peyroulet [Paris],
producer
Atelier de céramique Claude Aiello
[Vallauris, France], maker
Glazed earthenware
13 $\frac{1}{4}$ × 3 $\frac{1}{8}$"
34 × 8 cm

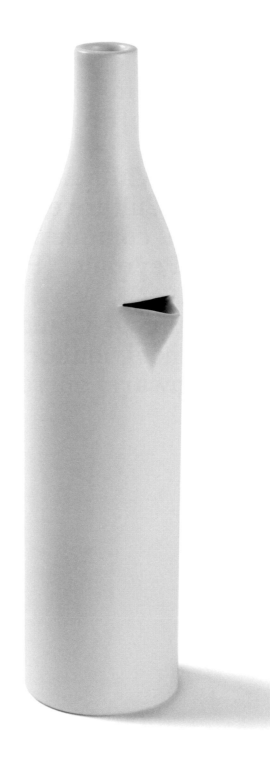

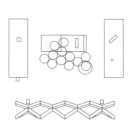

Coat hanger with mirror, 1999
Ronan Bouroullec [French, *1971]
Torique collection
Des designers à Vallauris,
Ministère de la Culture et de la
Communication, commissioner
Galerie Gilles Peyroulet [Paris],
producer
Atelier de céramique Claude Aiello
[Vallauris, France], maker
Glazed earthenware, mirror
8 × 5 ½"
20.5 ×14 cm

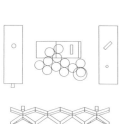

Desk, 2001
Erwan Bouroullec [French, *1976]
and Ronan Bouroullec [French, *1971]
Domeau & Pérès [France], producer
Corian, Connolly leather
29 $^7/_8$ × 57 $^1/_8$ × 21 $^3/_4$"
76 × 145 × 55 cm

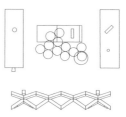

Grappe rug, 2001
Erwan Bouroullec [French, *1976]
and Ronan Bouroullec [French, *1971]
Galerie Kreo [France], producer,
and Les Fuses [Aubusson, France],
manufacturer
Woolmark velvet wool
$^3/_4$ × 63 $^3/_8$ × 42 $^1/_8$"
2 × 161 × 107 cm
12 circles, each ⌀ 30 cm

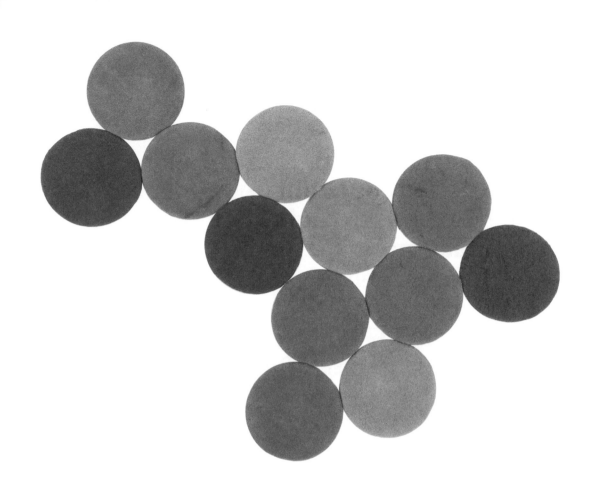

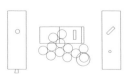

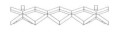

Trivet, 1999
Ronan Bouroullec [French, *1971]
Torique collection
Des designers à Vallauris,
Ministère de la Culture et de la
Communication, commissioner
Galerie Gilles Peyroulet [Paris],
producer
Atelier de céramique Claude Aiello
[Vallauris, France], maker
Glazed earthenware
1 $^3/_4$ × 7 $^7/_8$"
4.5 × 20 cm

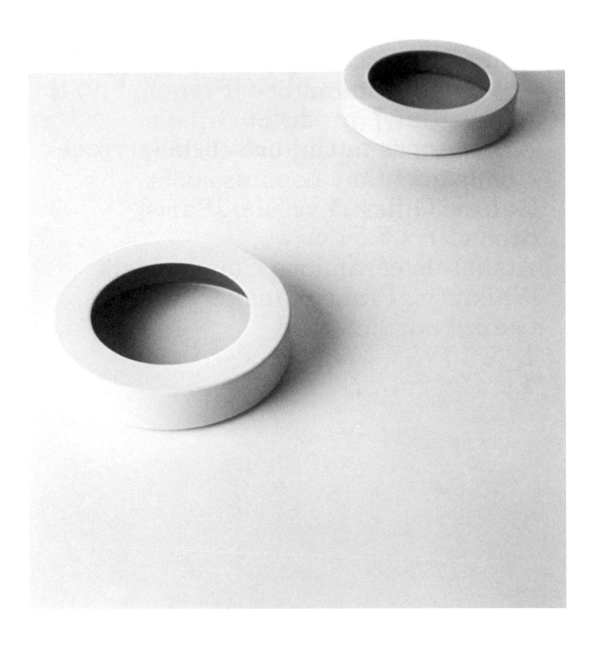
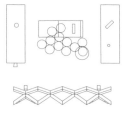

La Valise briefcase, 2003
Erwan Bouroullec [French, *1976]
and Ronan Bouroullec [French, *1971]
Magis [Italy], producer
ABS (Acrylonitrile-butadiene-styrene
copolymer)
12 $^1/_4$ × 14 $^5/_8$ × 3 $^1/_4$"
31.3 × 37 × 8.5 cm

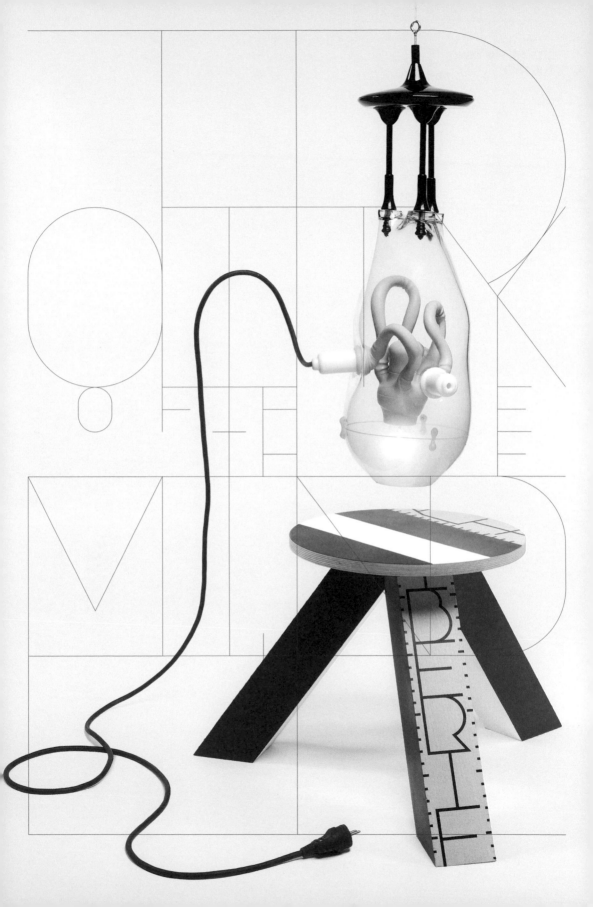

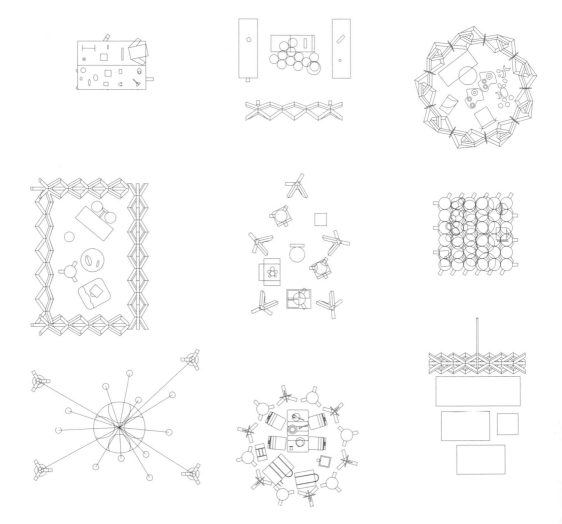

Introducing organic forms into inhabited space, the Prototype de luminaire lamp counters the social alienation symptomatic of the monumental urbanism of the new towns that sprang up in France beginning in the mid-1960s. These experimental, utopian, rationally planned cities were meant to allay the pressures placed on a growing urban population. Yet rather than integrate city dwellers into the built environment, the new towns effected greater individual isolation.

Prototype de luminaire lamp, 2001
Philippe Parreno [Algerian, *1964],
Pierre Huyghe [French, *1962],
and M/M (Paris)
Glass, aluminum, plastic, resin, paint,
electric wires
275 $^5/_8$ × 354 $^1/_4$" min.
700 × 900 cm min.

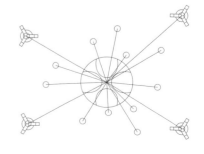

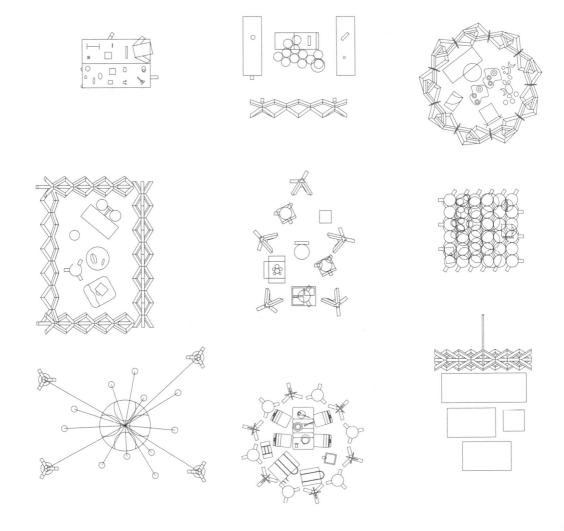

matali crasset's design practice
unsettles the notion of the "ideal
home." Her work encourages
individuals to take agency in shaping
the environments in which they live.
It is a lens through which to reconsider
the relationship between human
beings and design objects.

Chair, 2009
matali crasset [French, *1965]
Instant collection
Moustache [Paris], producer, 2010
Beech plywood
28 $^7/_8$ × 17 $^7/_8$ × 24 $^1/_4$"
73.5 × 45.5 × 61.5 cm
Table
26 $^1/_4$ × 55 $^1/_8$ × 27 $^5/_8$"
66.5 × 140 × 70 cm

Digestion nº1 cushions, 1998
matali crasset [French, *1965]
Digestion collection, 2000
Edra [Italy], manufacturer
Polyethylene bag filled
with polyurethane foam
21 $\frac{1}{4}$ × 25 $\frac{5}{8}$ × 11 $\frac{3}{8}$"
54 × 65 × 29 cm

Icipari radio, model, 1995
Philippe Starck [French, *1949],
artistic direction, and matali crasset
[French, *1965], design, for Tim Thom
Dream Products collection
Thomson, Telefunken [France],
manufacturer
Polyurethane resin, metal grill,
transfers, Plexiglas
$5 \frac{1}{2} \times 3 \frac{3}{4} \times 3 \frac{1}{8}$"
14 × 9.5 × 8 cm

MC02 mixing bowl,
from Essentiel de pâtisserie
[Baking Essentials], 2010
matali crasset [French, *1965]
Realized in collaboration
with Pierre Hermé
Alessi [Italy], producer
Stainless steel, silicone
ø 11 $^3/_4$"
ø 30 cm

Quand Jim monte à Paris,
hospitality column bed, 1995
matali crasset [French, *1965]
Domeau & Pérès [France],
manufacturer, 1998
Structure: tufted felt and bi-density
high-resilience foam
Mattress cover and inside: cotton
Open: 2 × 74 3/4 × 50"
5 × 190 × 127 cm
Folded: 74 3/4 × 13 3/8 × 13 3/8"
190 × 34 × 34 cm

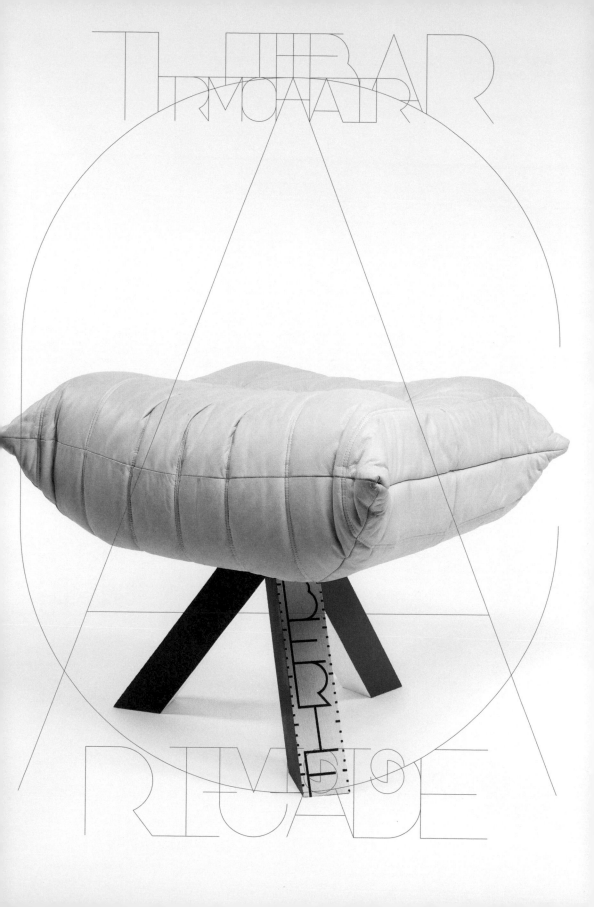

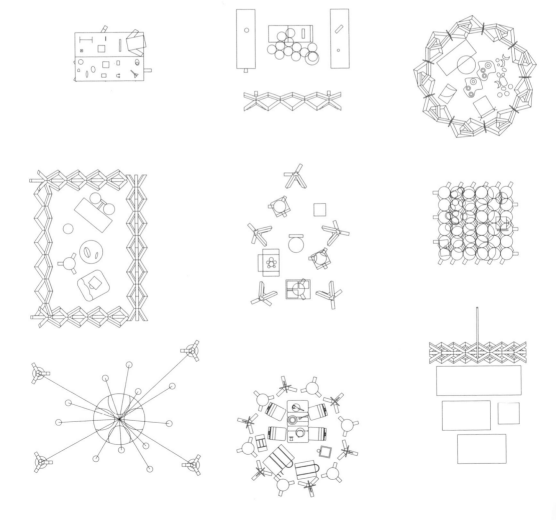

After the failure of the May 1968
"neo-revolution," in which students
and workers took to the streets
and created barricades around the
Latin Quarter, a politically engaged
formalism emerged in French design.
This bourgeois "armchair rebellion"
developed a new aesthetic of soft
anarchy, positioned uneasily between
the conflicting values of leftist
ideology and capitalism.

Elysée sofa, 1970
Pierre Paulin [French, 1927–2009]
Mangau–Alpha International
[France], producer
Mobilier national et Manufactures
des Gobelins, de Beauvais et de la
Savonnerie [France], commissioner
24 elements filled with foam screwed
to a wooden base, tubular structure,
tan leather lining
26 × 102 ³/₈ × 38 ¹/₄"
66 × 260 × 97 cm

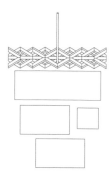

Loveseat and ottoman, 1973
Michel Ducaroy [French, 1925–2009]
Togo collection
Ligne Roset [France], manufacturer
Structure with variable density
polyurethane foam, padded quilted
removable cotton polyester cover
Various dimensions

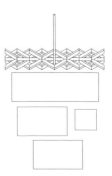

Yucca couch, 1980
Michel Ducaroy [French, 1925–2009]
Ligne Roset, Cinna [France],
manufacturer
Rubber foam, Arana leather
29 $\frac{1}{8}$ × 55 $\frac{1}{8}$ × 33 $\frac{1}{2}$"
74 × 140 × 85 cm

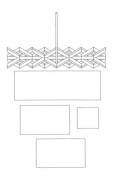

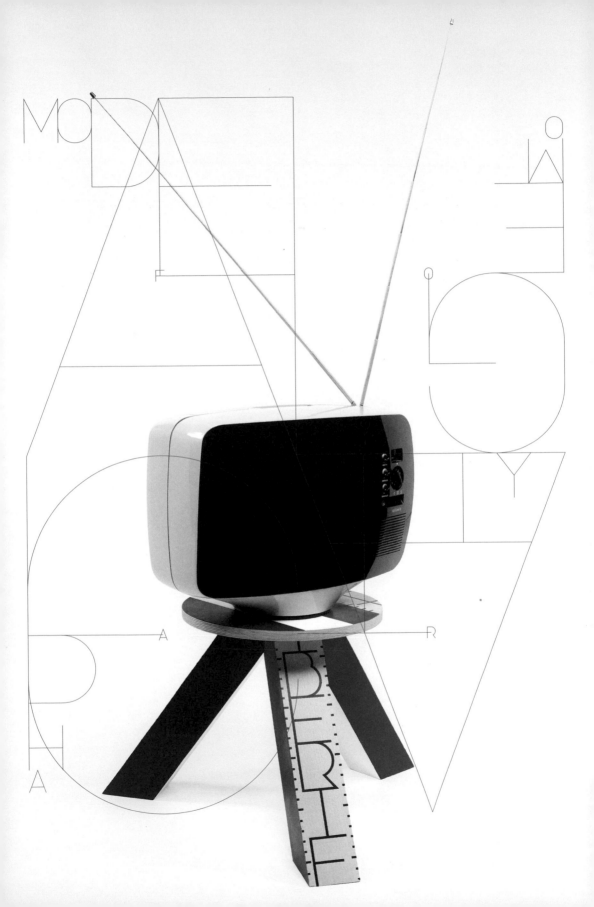

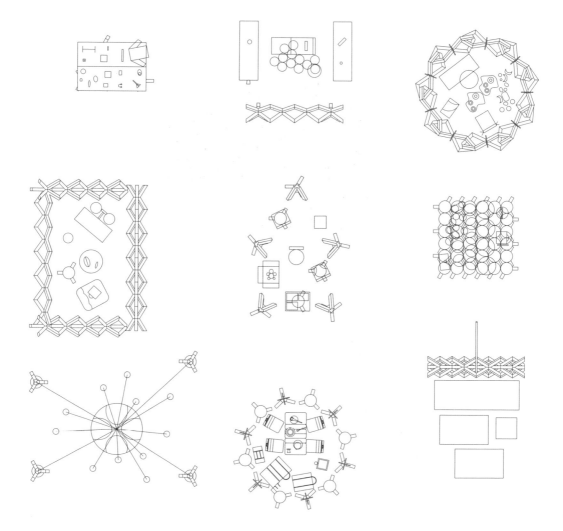

Modernist architects like Le Corbusier proposed rationalized norms of construction using defined measures to meet essential human needs.
In sharp contrast, French social utopian thought of the 1960s sought to expand the geography of human desire beyond the doctrine of minimal existence. Eminently mobile, and on occasion fully portable, Roger Tallon's designs resist the asceticism characteristic of modernist design. Working within an industrialized system of production, he has created objects that both span and enlarge physical space.

Stool, 1969
Roger Tallon [French, *1929]
Cryptogamme collection
Galerie Sentou [Paris], producer and
ERGO [Thailand], manufacturer, 2006
Polyester molded resin, Bultex foam,
Njord fabric
21 $^{3}/_{4}$ × ø 16 $^{1}/_{2}$"
55 × ø 42 cm

Module 400, 1965
Roger Tallon [French, *1929]
Galerie Lacloche [France], producer
First edition
Polished aluminum
60 $\frac{1}{4}$ × 15 $\frac{3}{8}$ × 15"
153 × 39 × 38 cm

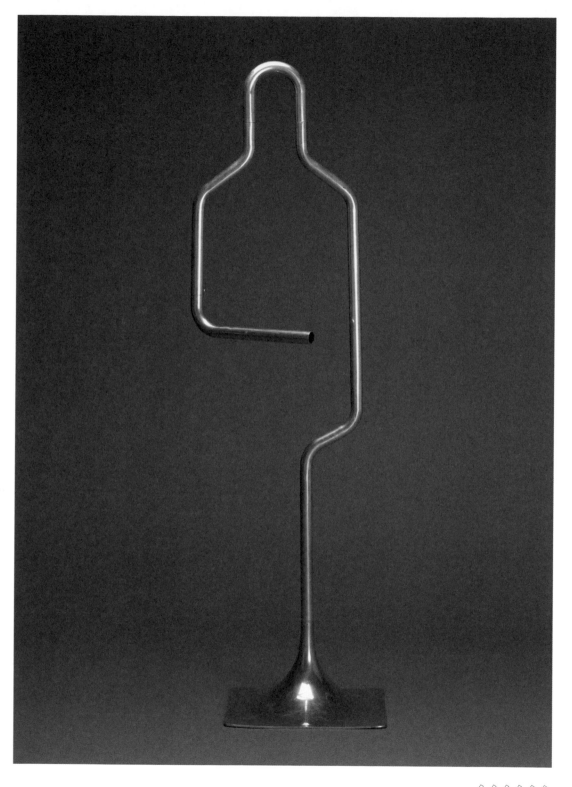

Pin Spot floor lamp, 1972
Roger Tallon [French, *1929]
Erco [Germany], manufacturer, 1973
Aluminum, plastic, lacquer, base in
painted aluminum, plastic mounting
system, plastic spot
64 ¼ × 23 ⅝ × 23 ⅝"
163 × 60 × 60 cm

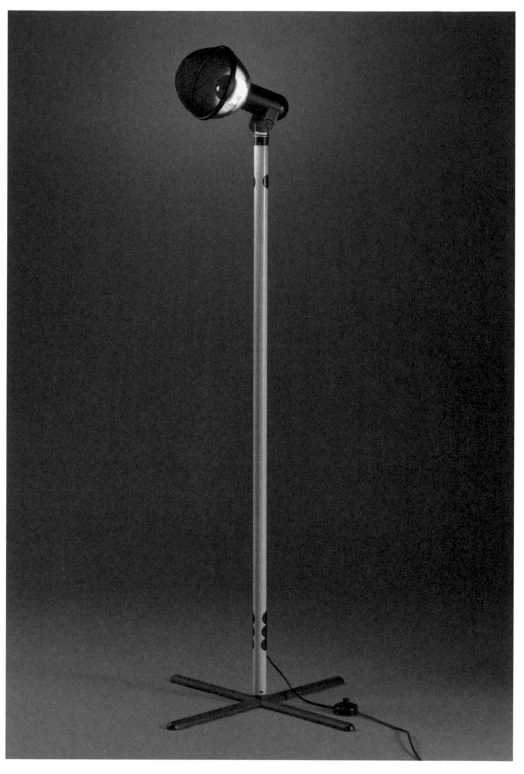

Portavia P111 portable television, 1963
Roger Tallon [French, *1929]
Téléavia [France], manufacturer, 1966
ABS (Acrylonitrile-butadiene-styrene
copolymer) case, acetobutyrate screen
15 $^3/_8$ × 21 $^1/_8$ × 11 $^3/_8$"
39 × 53.5 × 29 cm

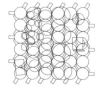

Terrines and plate, 2001
Roger Tallon [French, *1929]
Des designers à Vallauris,
Ministère de la Culture et de la
Communication, commissioner
Atelier Salvatore Oliveri / Atelier
de Moulage Sébastien Berthaud
[France], Galerie Sentou [France],
and Salvatore Oliveri
[Vallauris, France], makers
Glazed earthenware
Various dimensions

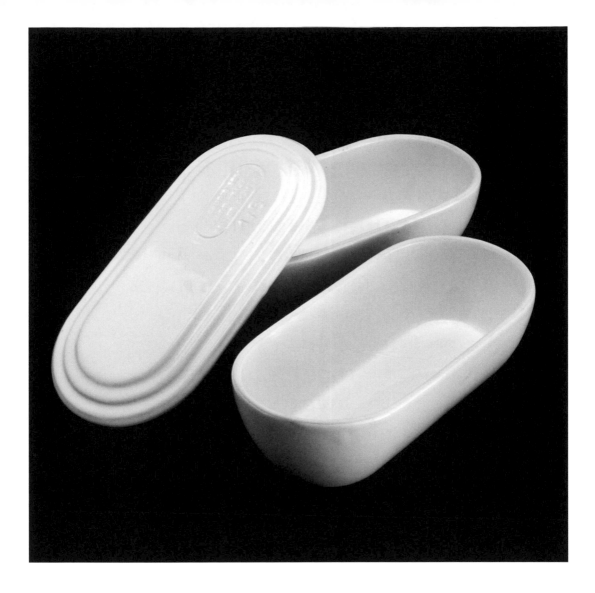

   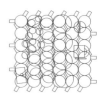

TS folding chair, 1967
Roger Tallon [French, *1929]
Galerie Sentou [France], producer,
after 1990
Beech plywood, varnish
30 $^1/_4$ × 19 $^3/_4$ × 19 $^3/_4$"
77 × 50 × 50 cm

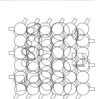

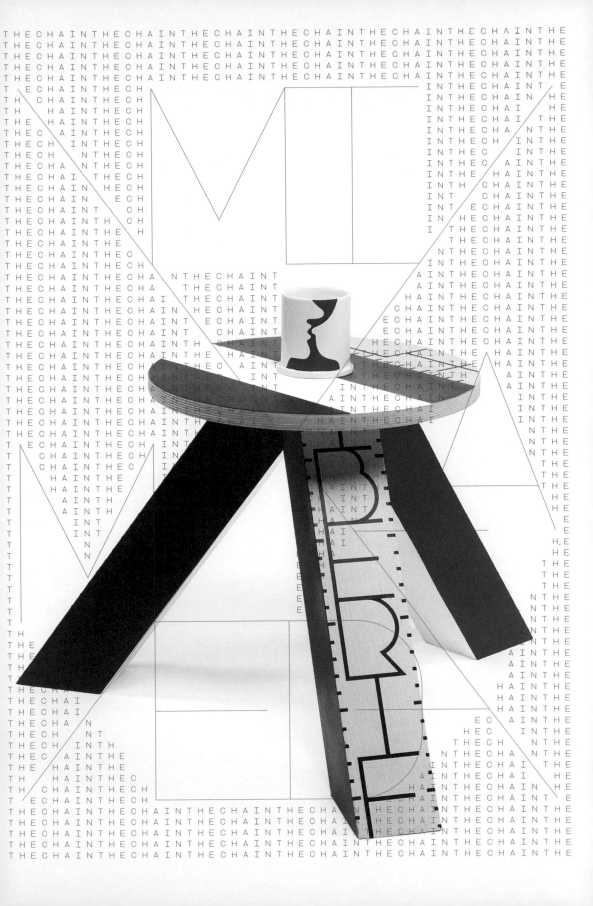

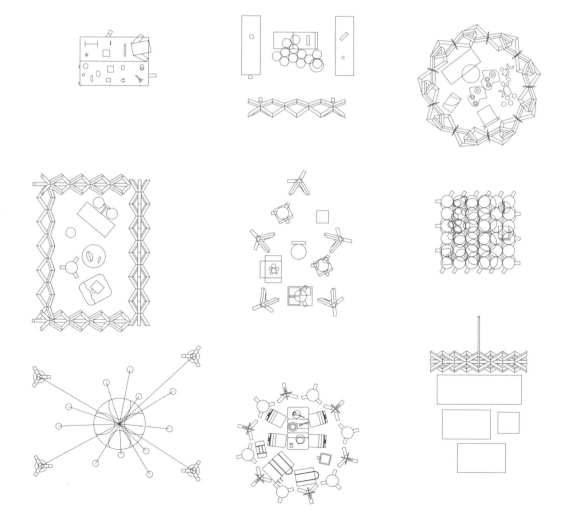

Informed by critiques of the
revolutionary claims of the 1960s
and the broadening of the accepted
canon of design history, designers
of the past twenty years have proposed
alternative approaches to design. Their
work engages themes—functionality,
irrationality, social consciousness,
and good taste, for instance—that
have colored the whole history of
French design.

Barbare chair, 1981
Garouste & Bonetti [French, est. 2001]:
Elizabeth Garouste [French, *1946]
and Mattia Bonetti [Swiss, *1952]
Galerie Neotu [Paris], producer
Iron with bronze antique patina,
cowhide, leather lace
45 ¹/₄ × 22 ³/₈ × 19 ¹/₂"
115 × 57 × 49.5 cm

Puzzle coffee table, 1970
Les Simonnet [French, est. 1970]:
Jean-Marie Simonnet [French, *1939]
and Marthe Simonnet [French, *1942]
Artists' edition, 1998
Polyester reinforced with fiberglass
18 ¹⁄₈ × 26 ³⁄₈ × 26 ³⁄₄"
46 × 67 × 68 cm

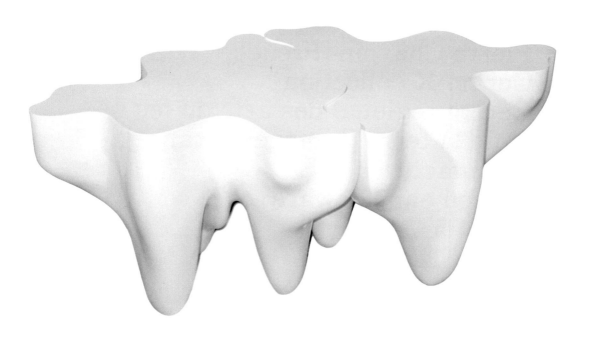

Vase, 2005
Pierre Charpin [French, *1962]
Ceram X collection
Centre régional des arts du feu
et de la terre [Limoges, France],
manufacturer
Glazed earthenware
8 $^7/_8$ × 5 $^3/_4$ × 2 $^3/_8$"
22.5 × 14.8 × 6 cm

Hyperspace seat, 2003
Jérôme Olivet [French, *1971]
Domeau & Pérès [France], producer
Painted fiberglass, resin
31 ½ × 14 ⅝ × 22"
80 × 37 × 56 cm

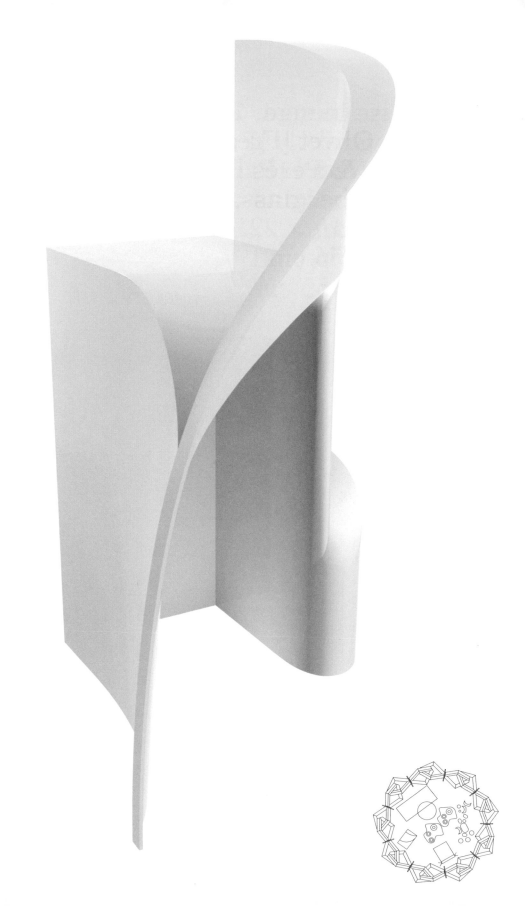

Pi chaise lounge, 1984
Martin Szekely [French, *1956]
Galerie Neotu [Paris], producer
Painted steel and aluminum,
leather, foam
37 $^3/_8$ × 49 $^1/_4$ × 21 $^3/_4$"
95 × 125 × 55 cm

Pi pedestal table, 1985
Martin Szekely [French, *1956]
Galerie Neotu [Paris], producer
Painted steel
29 ½ × ø 19 ¾"
75 × ø 50 cm

Vase #44, 2008
François Brument [French, *1979]
In-Flexions [France], producer,
and initial manufacturer
Polyamide powder sintering
Various dimensions

Dial D for Design
Alexandra Midal

"In the style of the Second Empire, the apartment became a sort of encasement, and the inhabitants were molded within the interior. At its birth, the detective novel enquired into relics and followed leads. The 'Philosophy of Furniture' and crime stories of Edgar Allan Poe make him the first physiognomist of the interior. The criminals in these early stories are neither gentlemen, nor apaches, but simple examples of the bourgeoisie."
(The Black Cat, The Tell-Tale Heart, William Wilson)
Walter Benjamin,
Paris: Capital of the 19th Century,
1939

On the shores of the Mediterranean in the south of France lies the city of Nice, emblematic capital of the French Riviera. This crossroads of cultures, a stone's throw from the Promenade des anglais, is where one of France's leading young designers, matali crasset, was commissioned to design her first hotel. Under her direction, the Hi Hotel was transformed from a cramped 1930s building to a thirty-eight-room retreat that revisits the conventional codes of hotel hospitality. Utilizing nine programmatic schemes, she restructured the building to create a gestalt experience: objects, furniture, and even architecture work together to create a design that fulfills and transcends its proper limits. The materialization of crasset's design results in almost the opposite of her original intent: an emergence of what she calls "ritual" or "empathy," terms whose meaning is difficult to render in current language. In the vocabulary of matali crasset, these terms are expressions of an inquiry that aims to deliver both the space and its inhabitant from the traditional codifications of the bourgeois.

In crasset's work, objects and space engage in a reciprocity and symbiosis that reverses the usual hierarchy between small and large that notoriously governs relations between design and other disciplines, such as architecture. Digestion n°1 (2000) is an example of this type of relationship. The work consists of a cube of polyurethane foam covered with a bag from Tati, a low-cost department store catering to the immigrant community, located in the north of Paris at Barbès-Rouchechouart, a working-class district. This cheap bag is quite easily recognizable by its unforgettable Vichy-check pattern. Parisians call it the Cabas Barbés.

Originally designed to meet the needs of busy, crowded spaces, such as bars and restaurants, and subsequently adapted for use in temporary exhibitions and events, Digestion n°1 became a project for the exhibition L'objet désorienté (The Disoriented Object) in 1999 at the Musée des arts décoratifs in Paris. Inspired by the fact that furniture rental suppliers offered such a meager selection, crasset, on a tight budget, created a seating system using columns of poufs. Covered in the easily recognizable pattern of the Tati bags, the columns are arranged in such a way that visitors might comfortably create their own space, a DIY experience and a personal invitation to interact with the space. The project was presented at the Satellite of the Milan Furniture Fair in 2001, and picked up by Edra, the Italian manufacturer, and the poufs were transformed into the collection that became known as Digestion.

Digestion is adaptable to a variety of uses. This popular ready-made marries the ordinary with extreme simplicity, while its malleable shape gives it a plasticity suitable for multiple uses. Simultaneously sofa, armless-chair, and/or wall, Digestion, with its emphasis on multi-functionality and impermanence, defies the ideal of domestic comfort that was so strongly established in nineteenth-century France by a new middle class. Motivated by consumption at any expense, moral or otherwise, this class was powerfully described by the novelists Zola, Balzac, and especially Flaubert.

matali crasset shatters the platitudes and profits of standardization and materialistic production by substituting the imaginary; one of her great achievements is her success in breaking-up, ripping, and drying-out the conventions of backward-looking and outdated design by releasing a new spaciographie.[1] The fiction and scenarios of the Hi Hotel show yet again this conceptual commitment. Take, for example, the room entitled Strates. Lying on the bed, the client has something besides a print of a Matisse or a Picasso to stare at: an open view of the bathroom. The space consists of two translucent-colored pods (one for the shower, the other for the toilet) perched atop several steps and fully visible to anyone in the room. The hotel room is thus functionally transformed first into a dressing room and then into a theater where clients might set the stage for their own fantasies.

Another design in the playful service of eroticized bodies is Ceram X (the title is a play on words combining "ceramics" and the "X" in pornography), a limited edition series of fifteen ceramics created by Pierre Charpin in 2005

[1]   Alexandra Midal, "Matali Crasset: Towards a New Design" in Matali Crasset: Works (New York-Milan: Rizzoli, 2012).

for the Centre régional des arts du feu et de la terre of Limoges. On the surfaces of the pieces, simplified forms of the genital and anal depict stylized erections, penetrations, sodomy, and other postures, with an effect that is enhanced by the choice of flat areas of bold colors.

By engaging the decorative, Charpin fits naturally into the demand for individual expression defended by a generation of Italian designers of the Memphis group and Studio Alchymia, especially Alessandro Mendini and Andrea Branzi, the Italian maestri with whom he feels in tune. To break away from the caricature they had made of the Modern movement, Branzi turned to the decorative as a critical space.

We have inherited an extremely narrow concept of decoration, one that is actually a by-product of painting; the very term "decorative" is often a synonym for the vulgarization of graphic and figurative devices, which are transformed in the repetitive processes of decoration into signs devoid of any cultural meaning. But this constricted view of ornament needs revising today, decorative thought has a modernity of its own and in some ways represents an extremely advanced type of aesthetic production even where experimental painting is concerned.[2]

Charpin appropriates a perspective on domestic decor associated with a dimension of eighteenth-century French political libertinism. Against the background of the views of eighteenth-century decorators like Georges Jacob,[3] who understood

[2]   Andréa Branzi, Italian New Wave Design: The Hot House
       (Cambridge: MIT Press, 1984), 116–117.
[3]   Georges Jacob was one of the most prominent furniture makers in Paris
       working in the early Neoclassical style, which later become associated with
Louis XVI. He produced carved, painted, and gilded furniture for all of the royal
residences.

domestic objects as a reflection of the social status of the nobility, the writings of the Marquis de Sade or Louis-Charles Fougeret Monbron interweave household furnishings and eroticism in order to slay the hypocrisies of a class-based society. Monbron's Le Canapé couleur de feu (The Flame-Colored Sofa, 1714) depicts the gallant story of a knight who, not being able to satisfy the desires of a witch, is transformed into a sofa that is moved from house to house, and on which members of the nobility and clergy frequently fornicate. The curse is broken after ten years of adventures, when true love is finally achieved.[4] In his correspondence from the Bastille prison, the Marquis de Sade related how objects, either in the details or the materials, can serve both to release and alleviate sexual energy.

[4]   Translator's note: Le Canapé couleur de feu is a libertine novel known at the time as an histoire gallante, which was in fashion in Europe from the sixteenth to the eighteenth centuries. Monbron traveled widely across Europe and even translated John Cleland's Fanny Hill into French.

Sade and Monbron, members of the nobility themselves, challenged the meanings attached to domestic objects by Jacob, and substituted instead an apologetics of eroticism using furniture and design.

Design and debauchery? This entry in French design seems too good to be true. We know the power of eroticism to reveal the hidden—in this case, a conception of design that escapes the dichotomy between good and evil. In the first published design history, Nikolaus Pevsner in 1936 presented function as the expression of morality, exemplified by the powerful virtue and nobility of William Morris and his successors.[5] Pevsner revisits the moralist position of writings by Augustus Pugin, Contrasts (1836) and True Principles of Christian Architecture (1841). Pevsner was

[5]   See Nikolaus Pevsner, Pioneers of the Modern Movement
       (London: Faber and Faber, 1936).

also inspired by Thomas Carlyle's
On Heroes and Hero Worship (1841),
which posits that the development of
civilization stems from the heroic
acts of individuals.

It is necessary to question the
historiography founded on a view
of design as the virtuous direction
of industrial production of useful,
functional objects. In Charpin's
pornographic figures or the
scenography of matali crasset's hotel
rooms, we see how well the designer
is able to inhabit other spaces beyond
virtue. To examine this perspective,
I invite you to come with me into
uncharted territory, and think through
the possibility of the reconciliation
between the figure of the designer and
the evil embodied by crime; to measure
together whether the horror of murder
accompanied by amorality might form
a new system beneficial to design.

The Dark Side of Design

A few years ago, scanning the bookshelves of one of my teachers from Princeton, I came across the work Serial Killers (1998) by Mark Seltzer. After flipping through a few pages about the infamous Winchester House, I discovered, quite by surprise, a "castle" built by H. H. Holmes in Chicago in 1886. Holmes was neither architect nor designer, but the plans for the building showed a surprising capacity to divert the most banal of spaces and objects into something more than functional. Seltzer explained that the building was at the intersection of two streets on a former waste ground left vacant by the great fire that ravaged Chicago in 1871. There Holmes built an imposing house that his neighbors nicknamed "the castle." Each of the floors had around thirty-six rooms and the ground floor included a drugstore, a restaurant,

and even a jewelry store—an effort
on Holmes's part to prove himself a
respectable member of society. Lurking
behind this bourgeois veneer, however,
was a labyrinth of odds and ends
and everything in between: narrow
passages, staircases, doors and secret
rooms; hidden passageways and trap
doors; a windowless room that could
be emptied of air; even a soundproof
feature—ingenious devices. Upon
further, closer inspection, the project
unveils the morbidity of a person who
has been documented as the first
American serial killer. This "castle,"
completed by Holmes in 1893, was built
for the unique purpose of executing
criminal acts and was full of devices
essential to that cause: ovens, hatches,
and other "machines" allowing for the
comfortable and discreet performance
of murder.

In contrast to other buildings of the
time, the distribution of different

architectural parts created disorganized spaces, and was primarily based on a proliferation of technological devices meant to serve deadly objectives. Form distinctly followed function as Holmes welcomed hell into home.

Similar connections between murder and design reveal a hidden pin in the history of modern design. The field of design history has been built on Pevsner's misunderstanding of the relationship between function and virtue. Since, by convention, the designer must follow the rules of function, then breaking these boundaries is a crime.

The design historian Reyner Banham was the first to pick apart the virtuous history of design as stated by Pevsner. For Banham:

The history of the mechanization
of environmental management is
a history of extremists, otherwise
most of it would never have
happened. The fact that many of
these extremists were not registered,
or otherwise recognized as
architects, in no way alters the
magnitude of the contribution they
have made to the architecture of
our time. Perhaps finding such men
a proper place in the history
of architecture will be some help
in resolving the vexed problems
of finding their proper place
in the practice of architecture.[6]

"Murder like love is an art," is
an affirmation claimed by Mark
Lamphere, the young architect in Fritz
Lang's film Secret Beyond the Door
(1948). This bold idea is echoed in
Alfred Hitchcock's film Rope (1948),

[6] Reyner Banham, The Architecture of the Well-Tempered Environment
(Chicago: University of Chicago Press, 1984), 16–17.

in which two young men kill a friend for the beauty of the gesture. To strangle their friend, they use an ordinary rope that one of them then hides in his jacket pocket. The film continues as the bride and the victim's family come to dinner with the two friends, and a buffet is prepared on a trunk containing the body of the deceased. Upon leaving, the victim's father takes with him a bunch of books tied with the same rope used a few hours earlier to strangle his son.

Hitchcock's story comes from an incident that took place in the United States during the 1920s. Following the reading of Thomas De Quincey's 1827 "On Murder Considered As One Of The Fine Arts," two students from the University of Chicago, Leopold and Loeb, wanted to see if crime could turn them into artists, and without further ado they killed one of their friends. Hitchcock emphasizes slippage of function: the same box used for storing things, in itself banal, becomes a tomb, while the rope is used to tie together the books after it is used for strangling. Hitchcock's thriller rests on a respect for objects and users, even if both become morally compromised or misappropriated. Unlike the modular function that generally organizes design and notably the work of matali crasset, the idea here is that while the function is essentialy the same (a rope can be used to encircle tightly both books and a throat), there is a difference in intent, motive, the character of the user, etc. We might ask ourselves if any ordinary, or even extraordinary, object can be defined or thought of in the same way when certain acts or uses take it beyond its established function.

I would like to show that an investigation into the history of design gives rise to a parallel between

designer and criminal, and that
the practice of design goes beyond
the good vs. evil dichotomy initially
proposed by Pevsner. There are a
collection of famous precedents,
including De Quincey's, in which
the writer invents a brotherhood,
the "Society of Connoisseurs in
Murder," whose members, "the zealot
assassins," treat this shocking and
immoral activity aesthetically.
De Quincey writes:

As it is impossible to hammer
anything out of it for moral
purposes, let us treat it aesthetically,
and see if it will turn to account
in that way. Such is the logic of a
sensible man, and what follows?
We dry up our tears, and have the
satisfaction, perhaps, to discover
that a transaction, which, morally
considered, was shocking, and
without a leg to stand upon,
when tried by principles of Taste,

turns out to be a very meritorious performance.[7]

Oscar Wilde described in The Picture of Dorian Gray (1890) a body intact and eternal, the protagonist hiding at the sight of all the evil and dark traces of the murderer on the portrait, which shows the progression of deformity. In the face of the public reaction to such a monster as Gray, Wilde reponded: "There is no such thing as a moral or an immoral book. Books are well written, or badly written. That is all."[8] Gray's duplicity becomes visible only at the moment that he defaces his portrait. Wilde, consequently, does not completely get rid of the evidence; he hides and relegates it inside a work of art.

I use the premise that investigation

[7]   Translator's note: This essay, first published by Thomas De Quincey in Blackwood's Magazine in 1827, is a fictional account addressed to a gentleman's club. It led him to write "A Second Paper on Murder, Considered As One Of The Fine Arts" in 1834 and a "Postscript" in 1854.
[8]   Wilde added his preface in 1891, when the novel—which had originally appeared as a serial—was first published as a book.

into design can yield unseen or unexpected evidence to delve into the collection from the Centre national des arts plastiques (National Center for Visual Arts, or CNAP), and through these investigations explore Exhibit A: Liberty, Equality, and Fraternity. Together we will unravel the threads of this history.

The discovery of a possible link between design and crime—whether it is a violation of the laws of function or the violation committed by a killer like Holmes—is perplexing. The practice of Holmes, for example, provides a window onto design as an extreme, violent, nightmarish practice. Since I am exploring the figure of the murderer as a designer in extremis and banal objects turned into murder weapons, nothing seems more appropriate than to take on the role of detective, my alias for the occasion, in which I wrap my thoughts and speculations.

I suggest we attempt to go through an examination, with its deadlocks and breakthroughs, and reconnect the roles of investigator and critic, since "being a critic means that one is ready to become a criminal, or at least that one is ready to actively look at crime."[9] Both reunite pieces of evidence, trace clues, and reconstruct the events of the past.

This parallel is particularly troubling in light of the passage that I quoted by Walter Benjamin at the beginning of this text. The detective is inseparable from the interior and the interior inseparable from the detective. Within the crime novel there is a dual investigation, and the detective can give way to another inhabitant, both historian and investigator, whose very home is the scene of the crime.

[9] Jean-Michel Rabaté, Étant donnés: 1.l'art, 2. le crime – La modernité comme
     scène du crime (Dijon: Presses du réel, 2010), 25. A variant of this work has
been published in English as Given, 1° Art 2° Crime: Modernity, Murder, and Mass
Culture (Portland: Sussex Academic Press, 2007).

Disquieting Zones

In 1994 the French mail order
catalogue 3 Suisses proposed for a
little less than one-thousand dollars
a build-it-yourself house, designed by
no less than Philippe Starck! A short
time after placing my order, I received
a wooden case in which I found a video
cassette, schematic diagrams, and
plans for framing, carpentry, heating,
plumbing, electricity, a notebook, a
hammer, and a French flag (to install
in the pinnacle when the house is
finally built). The surface area of this
wooden contraption measures 867
square feet with a corridor of 525
square feet, and has a large room on
the ground floor and a first floor.

While snooping around, I discovered
that one of the few examples of these
houses ever built was used in the last
scenes of a film by Yvan Attal, Ils se
marièrent et eurent beaucoup d'enfants

(released in English as And They Lived Happily Ever After, 2004). The house goes far beyond the functionality associated with the architecture itself and is transformed into a cave of the psyche of three unhappily coupled forty-something men. On a psychological and symbolic level, the undecorated house crystallizes, catalyzes, and transmutes the angst of the three men.

In so far as Starck's house might possibly be a "crime scene," the subject is worth exploring further. Let's look at how the tormented soul of the living is rooted in the domestic. The concept has been revisited in The Architectural Uncanny (1992) by the historian Anthony Vidler. The uncanny, or Unheimlichkeit, is an idea first posed by Sigmund Freud, indicating the fusion of the familiar and uncomfortably strange that one sometimes experiences in the

refuge of the home. Alfred Hitchcock
achieved just this very state of being
in narrating the trailer for Psycho
(1960), in which an ordinary house is
gradually transformed into the scene
of a crime.

The home of Starck renews the
question of the impact of architecture
on the mind, its ability to produce
sensations and to instill emotional
states that in turn affect the behavior
of people. In Attal's film, Starck's house
belongs to a tradition of spatialization
of affect. The house represents a
corollary and an acting-out of the
psychological state of each couple as
they attempt to overcome an existential
crisis. It is a space that creates the
unconscious mood of its occupants.

This relationship between domestic
space and feeling is familiar from the
heyday of the French decorative arts.
The invention of "decorative landscape"

in 1891 by the critic Alphonse Germain underscored the transformative power of décor by drawing a model of a pastoral house, symbolized by an "oasis of green," an image suggesting an idealized refuge. Germain recommended these colors and shapes as a means of refreshing the body and mind of the "weary intellectual." What was not yet called design was the essential element in a decorative scheme able to shape the minds and souls of its inhabitants.[10] The French reviews of the period, Art et décoration and L'Art décoratif, gave weight to this notion through the expression "psychology of the parts." The idea of psychological space has also been brilliantly explored by Deborah Silverman in Art Nouveau in Fin-de-Siecle France (1992), an anaylsis comparing the "new psychology" and the Art Nouveau movement.

[10] Joyce Henri Robinson, "Hi Honey, I'm Home: Weary (Neurasthenic)
    Businessmen and the Formulation of a Serenely Modern Aesthetic" in
Not At Home, ed. Christopher Reed (London: Thames & Hudson, 1996), 98–112.

In the same era, the two brothers
Edmond and Jules Goncourt explained
that one of their principal reasons
for publishing books was so that
they could make enough money to
redecorate their hotel particulier in the
Rococo style, an attempt to provoke a
"febrile state" by playing with internal
harmony and nervous vibrations. The
brothers' interest reflects the influence
of the clinician on the design of private
space and suggests that another
depiction of the psyche could be found
in the inner states of being, which in
turn finds considerable resonance in
architecture and the city.

This mental construct that a house
resonates with the feelings of
its inhabitant combined with the
destruction and violence of the First
World War to prepare the way for
the genre cinema of the 1920s. In
the American horror film The Old
Dark House (1932) by James Whale,

architecture plays the role of instilling
dramatic tension. On a psychological
and symbolic level, the house becomes
the catalyst of the characters. The
same construction is found in the
films of the German Expressionist
movement, particularly in Waxworks
(1924) by Paul Leni, and takes the
leading role in The Cabinet of Dr.
Caligari (1920), where the architecture
and the cardboard houses give form
to the intensity of feelings shaking the
protagonists. Out of the archetypes
that accompanied the technological
explosion and the standardization of the
industrial revolution, a new individual
is born, one who is at once modern
and psychological, and who is capable
of becoming one with the home. The
body is not limited by its physicality
and extends into space, finding its
counterpart in the house designed by
Starck, which becomes a canvas for the
physiognomies and tormented psyches
of its inhabitants in Attal's film.

Lost in thought even if I know
I need to advance in my new job
as a detective, I realize that inside
my briefcase from 3 Suisses, oddly
enough, the hammer that was there
when I opened it is now gone. But
I'm the only one here, so who took it?
And why? Faced with my subject,
I can't help but wonder: could the
same hammer used to pound a nail
also be used to commit a crime?
And where could such a crime
be committed?

In France it is forbidden to build
a house larger than 170 square
meters (1,830 square feet) without
the signature of a certified architect,
a piece of legislation that dates from
the fascist Vichy regime. Starck's
exploit, which proposes to dispense
with the architect by keeping the
project smaller than the legal limit,
is a daring act in view of power
relations between architecture

and design. It is a challenge to the
hiearchy privileging architect over
designer that was anchored in the
emergence of the Modern movement.

This situation, in fact, was already
described in 1895 by M. H. Baillie
Scott as follows: "It is difficult for
the architect to draw a fixed line
between the architecture of a house
and the furniture. The conception of
an interior must necessarily include
the furniture, which is to be used
in it, and this naturally leads to the
conclusion that the architect should
design chairs and tables as well
as the house itself."[11] Claimed by
architects with a vision of unitary
design, "architecture concentrated"
rested on the idea that the inside and
outside are inseperable: "The inside
and the outside of a modern structure
are regarded as one thanks to the

[11]   Quoted in Marian Page, Furniture designed by architects
       (London and New-York: Whitney Library of Design, Watson-Guptill
Publications, Architectural Press Ltd., 1983), 8.

technological development of building with large sheets of glass, and the aesthetic development of sensing objects simultaneously from many vantage points."[12]

In Mechanization Takes Command (1948), the historian Sigfried Giedion wrote about the redefinition of the boundaries between architecture and design beginning in the 1920s. With the decline of the profession of interior designer and its replacement by the architect, "the architects superseded the decorative artist as the author of new furniture types." Giedion added: "Looking at the present-day trends, we commented in 1931, one sees that the decorator has lost all prestige as a designer of furniture. Almost every important inspiration comes from architects now setting standards for the future. Today the slightest item of furniture must participate in the new

[12]   Peter Blake, The Master Builders (New York: Knopf, 1960), 7.

architectural spirit, a fusion that the architect takes quite for granted."[13]

The supremacy of the architect capable of building a hyper-interior is one of the characteristics of the Modern movement. For proof one only has to look at Charlotte Perriand. Although she trained at the École de l'union centrale des arts décoratifs in Paris, and exhibited with the Société des artistes décorateurs before becoming one of the founding members in 1929 of the l'Union des artistes modernes, she has always been considered and presented as an architect and not as a designer.[14] This aspect of design is far from being a French singularity: it is also found across the Atlantic in the American couple Charles and

[13] Die Bauwelt n° 33 (1933) quoted by Siegfried Giedion in Mechanization Takes
      Command, a Contribution to an Anonymous History (New York: Norton, 1975), 484.
[14] Yvonne Brunhammer states: "Charlotte Perriand addressed the concerns
      of the relationship between humans and the environment, between actions and
objects, and the resulting harmony, not only more frequently than the architects of
her generation but also better. See Brunhammer, Charlotte Perriand: Un art de Vivre
(Paris: Musée des arts décoratifs, 1985), 77. For more on Perriand, see her Une Vie
de création (Paris: Odile Jacob, 1988).

Ray Eames, who primarily designed furniture even though most considered their praxis architecture and not design. From Eames to Jean Nouvel and from Andrea Branzi to Greg Lynn, it is easy to trace the succession of architects who questioned the foundation of this globalized concept of architecture, which was attempting to swallow everything in its path. Starck's project also challenges the modernist domination of the architect.

Don't be fooled by Starck's house: he reverses the current protocol by substituting the designer for the architect. With this act he has committed murder.

When we begin to speak of crime, of operating beyond the laws that regulate human society, whether literally or metaphorically, we confront the violence of function represented by the murder of twenty-seven persons by H. H. Holmes. But the category of crime is varied and vast. For there are also violations against good taste, a subject addressed by the Austrian architect Adolf Loos in his essay, Ornament and Crime (1908). So bad taste or serial murder, what matters is that both are crimes.[15]

To really delve into the complexity of the history of modern design, one must be prepared to open an investigation. The case remaining unsolved, the trail running cold, how do we reopen it? The text History and Psychiatry, originally published in Architectural Review (May 1960), provided Banham the opportunity to remind the modern generation of a "zone of silence." Under the spotlight of crime, which Banham is accused of unveiling, the accursed part of design is revealed.

[15] See Hal Foster, Design and Crime (2002).

Mysteries, Poltergeist, and MacGuffin

As far as I can see, my investigation remaining genuinely unresolved, all that matters now is the trembling. If crime, my leitmotif, holds any power, it requires that everything be reviewed according to new parameters that defy morality. Next to the statement of heroic design (Pevsner) or the glorious and anonymous (Giedion), Starck's house, like Holmes' before him, reveals the accursed legacy of design. And from this fatal perspective, I must return to the design of objects, the ultimate evidence.

Let us consider the Kelly bag from Hermès. Based on a pouch originally used by cavalrymen, it was launched commercially as the sac à dépêches in 1935. The story of how the bag found its current namesake comes a posteriori. In 1956, in the photo section of Life magazine, the bag appeared in the hands of Princess Grace of Monaco, who was using it to cover something as she was getting into a limousine. In fact the young princess was pregnant, and the duchy of Monaco had not yet officially announced it. The object itself was baptized with and thereafter known by Princess Grace's maiden name, transforming a very private matter into a very public spectacle twenty-one years after the bag's creation.

The Kelly became a sacrosanct feature of French design during the 1950s, a time when France established the foundations of national industrial production by strengthening links between French industry and furniture design. Driven by the economic boom of the post-war period, France, like many countries in Western Europe, responded to consumer demand by developing its capacity for mass production.

Andrea Branzi has argued that this strategy follows from the way in which Europe faced the economic crisis of the 1930s, when it chose a path opposed to the American model of individual consumption based on free-market principles. In contrast to the American model, Europeans rooted their industrial development in a regulated market, making social engagement the prerogative of the designer. For Branzi, the Western European position differs from the American in that it was based on an ideological theorem of integrating standardization, not as a means of production, but as the central social determinant of the definition of design and as the embodiment of progress. With the adoption of the Marshall Plan, France received not only American financial support, but also its particular free market ideology, characterized in part by the idea that the mass production of consumer goods was a symbol of the good life.

The Merchandise Mart in Chicago, established in the late 1940s, is an example of this American dynamism, with its multiplication of operations of seduction advanced by the precepts of "Good Design" developed by Edgar Kaufman Jr., of the Museum of Modern Art. The Merchandise Mart promoted the idea that good design actively participates in the revival of the domestic economy, expressing support for a nation rather than simply furnishing it. In other words, design was assigned the task of establishing an image that reflects the happiness of a nation; design became both political and patriotic.

"The Kitchen Debate," as it was called by the New York Times, took place in front of the press at the American National Exhibition in Moscow. Before a display of household appliances there stood the incongruous figures of the Vice President of the United

States, Richard Nixon, and the Soviet Premier, Nikita Khrushchev. In the heart of the Cold War, the leaders of the two largest world powers were conversing next to a model kitchen, and each was arguing for the benefits of the domestic production of consumer goods. Underlying their "household" conversation were suggestions of a parallel between domestic appliances and the arms race. "Would it not be better to compete in the relative merits of washing machines than in the strength of rockets. Is this the kind of competition you want?" Nixon asked. Khrushchev replied, "Yes that's the kind of competition we want. But your generals say: 'Let's compete in rockets. We are strong and we can beat you.' But in this respect we can also show you something."[16]

While Nixon praised the values of the free market, Khrushchev advocated

[16] "The Two Worlds: A Day-Long Debate," in the New York Times, July 25, 1959.

those of communism. This famous encounter between two political and economic visions shows how, above all, the issue of design is primarily ideological. If America promotes the idea of well-being accessible to all, and consumer goods embody this principle, then the policy of encouraging consumption was based on the ideal of a comfortable home made so by the furnishings that go with it. By accepting American financial aid, France slowly adopted the same ideals. Despite continued clashes over rationing, the end of the Second World War brought with it a sustained wave of optimism. French designers found freedom in the use of "free form," organic and curvilinear, drawing heavily on American Abstract Expressionism. Both culturally and symbolically, design had become a laboratory.

But in the 1950s, torn between
the reactivation of the Bauhaus in
Dessau and the nostalgia of savoir-
faire, and between the social value
of standardization and the value
of quality craftsmanship, French
designers were mostly concerned with
the difficulty they faced in reconciling
industry and quality. Within this
idealization of durable and unique
objects that were to fulfill the promise
of democracy and the quality of
standardization, there emerged a neo-
positivist design project that engaged
with reality. This momentum rang the
death knell of modernity.

This end is heralded by Robert
Aldrich's Kiss Me Deadly (1955).
The plot revolves around a struggle
between thugs and the ever-popular
private investigator Mike Hammer.
Everyone is trying to get their hands
on a mysterious suitcase, elegantly
sheathed in leather and narrow

buckled straps, its contents unknown to its pursuers. The film ends in a radioactive apocalypse. Modernity has reached its apogee: the mystery of the coveted black box.

The architecture critic Reyner Banham, in "Black Box, the Secret Profession of Architecture," posits that architecture is a mysterious modum architectum, like a black box that cannot be opened and instead can only "give hints about the content." The black box can "continue as a conspiracy of secrecy, immune from scrutiny, but perpetually open to the suspicion, among the general public, that there may be nothing at all inside the black box except a mystery for its own sake."[17]

Suspicions and tensions reach an apex at the end of the Aldrich film

[17] Reyner Banham, "Black Box" first appeared in New Statesman & Society, October 12 1990, and again in A Critic Writes, Selected Essays by Reyner Banham (Berkeley: University of California Press, 1999), 299.

when the contents of the mysterious object are revealed to be a nuclear bomb. The black box of design, in which the functional and morbid are joined, holds its share of mystery. It is no coincidence that my investigation began with Grace Kelly, the heroine of To Catch a Thief (1955), and Rear Window and Dial M for Murder (both in 1954). These three criminal intrigues are all served by the MacGuffin.

Alfred Hitchcock explained the narrative function of the MacGuffin in the following popular anecdote: "Two passengers are in a train from London to Edinburgh when one says to another: Excuse me, sir, but how strange that package looks that you placed in the rack above your head? —Oh that's a MacGuffin!—What's a MacGuffin?—Well, it's a device used to catch the lions in the mountains of Scotland.—But there are no lions in the mountains of Scotland.—In that case, it's not a MacGuffin."[18]

We will never fully understand what a MacGuffin is, rebuffing any attempt we might make at rationalizing fiction, just as we will not be able to define what inherently constitutes design. Just as the MacGuffin sets a narrative in motion, its mystery an opening to the imagination, the black box of design initiates the passage from rational to speculative fiction, routing any explanation, and substitutes creative license for the rationalist narrative that is usually associated with the virtues of standardized production.

A strange materiality surfaces when design acts like a MacGuffin, sliding from function to fiction. In the same way that the emergence of ghost stories was usually associated with complex,

[18] François Truffaut, Le Cinéma selon Alfred Hitchcock
(Paris: Robert Laffont, 1966), 112

if not conflicting, relationships, and ran parallel to the technological progress of the nineteenth century, spectra disturb domestic technology and betray the incomprehensibility of nature. In its own way, design revisits the principle of the phantom.

The dialectic between design and spectra determines the framework of Serge Brussolo's Procédure d'évacuation immédiate des musées fantômes (The Procedure of Urgent Evacuation for Ghost Museums, 1987). The novel describes a deserted post-nuclear Paris without any energy resources. To solve the energy problem, scientists convert the souls of the dead into electricity. At the same time, a scientist by the name of Gregori Mikofsky, creator of the "Destroy" project, discovers that the destruction of objects, including works of art, creates an exploitable energy wave called "Y".

One thing is certain: objects contain a mass of energy that stocks the memory of daily use; cold, heat, shock.... All the experiments that we have conducted show that the voluntary assassination of an object or even its negligent destruction leaves intact a mass of energy waves called Y. It is here, following death, that the occultist speaks again of phantoms. They tell us that violent death leaves behind it unsatisfied specters.[19]

Setting aside the question of fact or fiction, if the world were as Brussolo describes, could we not consider that objects might come under the influence of ghosts? In addition to bearing her name, might the Hermès bag, by virtue of its link to Princess Grace, possess and personify a ghostly presence?

[19] Serge Brussolo, Procédure d'évacuation immédiate des musées fantômes (Paris: Denoël, 1987), 39.

The Bouloum chair, designed by
Olivier Mourgue for the French
Pavilion in Osaka in 1970, can
be understood in such a way. It is
frequently remarked upon from a
technical perspective for its innovative
use of foam cover and colored jersey
upholstery, a practice opposed to the
orthogonality praised by the previous
generation.[20] The jersey upholstery
is part of the development and use
of virgin materials that brushes
against the history of architecture
and makes a break with earlier
practices.

Just as the Bauhaus designers
before them turned to metal tubing
as a material suited to standardization,
cost efficiency, and democratization,
designers of the 1960s exploited recent
technological advances in plastics.
Roland Barthes, in Mythologies,

[20] It is difficult to identify who first succeeded in implementing this technical
    innovation: Pierre Paulin's Mobilier National (1967), Verner Panton's Vision 2
(1970), or Olivier Mourgue's Djinn (1965)

described the emblematic alchemy of plastics, which have neither intrinsically predetermined color nor form:

> Despite having names of Greek shepherds (Polystyrene, Phenoplast, Polyvynile, Polyethylene), plastic, the products of which have just been gathered in an exhibition, is in essence the stuff of alchemy. At the entrance of the stand, the public waits in a long queue in order to witness the accomplishment of the magical operation par excellence: the transmutation of matter. An ideally-shaped machine tubulated and oblong...effortlessly draws, out of a heap of greenish crystals, shiny and fluted.... At one end, raw, telluric matter, at the other, the finished, human object; and between these two extremes, nothing....[21]

[21] Roland Barthes, "Le plastique," Mythologies (Paris: Seuil, 1957), 159–160.
Translator's Note: In English, "Plastic," Mythologies (London: Vintage, 2009), 117.

Through these transformations, plastic takes on all forms. Mimicry is both its strength and its weakness. Barthes was not the only one to emphasize what he called Fregolisme (or the delusion of doubles) surrounding plastic. Architect Ezio Manzini has also examined what makes this troubling material both complex and hybrid: "Plastics are like Zelig, the Woody Allen character who is transformed according to the circumstances, taking on the most varied faces."[22] Just like Zelig, who takes on the appearance and behavior of other people, plastic performs any transformation assigned to it.

The ephemeral, alchemical nature of plastic, together with its affordability and its association with consumer satisfaction, enabled designers in the 1960s to uphold the social values of the

[22] Ezio Manzini, La Materia dell' invenzione (Milan: Arcadia, 1986);
      French translation by A. Pilia and J. Demarcq, La Matière de l'invention
(Paris: Éditions du Centre Pompidou / Centre de création industrielle, 1989), 66.

Modern movement while undermining its metaphysics. The immutability of physical laws, standing for something timeless and inalienable, was destroyed by the arrival of new materials like plastic and jersey.

Wouldn't it also be legitimate to analyze the Bouloum chair as Barthes "read" plastic, as a graphic sign? In structuralist terms, the chair signifies the supine position of the sitter. This analysis would also accomplish a coherent reading of the cultural transformations of the 1960s, when sitting at length and almost at ground level embodied conversation. The Bouloum manifestly encourages the baby boom generation to defy the conventions and practices of their middle-class parents. Nevertheless, all convincing analyses aside, nothing can take away from the fact that the Bouloum is indeed quite similar in appearance to the chalk silhouette

drawn by police investigators at
a crime scene.

Thus the traces of the body transform
domestic space into a crime scene,
making it not just fertile but also
suspect. It is owing precisely to this
fact that Walter Benjamin argued: "At
its birth, the detective novel enquired
into relics and followed leads."[23] It is
doubtlessly for this reason that, beyond
technological exploits, the explosion of
plastics, jersey, and inflatable materials
in the 1960s can be looked at through
the prism of ectoplasm, the formless
and invisible spirits that live inside
structures and give them volume.

After evoking these ghostly specters,
the deceased survive in objects. The
possibility of murdering the architect
so that the designer might build the
house informs and encourages astral

[23] Walter Benjamin, Paris, capitale du XIXe siècle, in Das Passagen-Werk
      (Frankfurt am Main, Suhrkamp Verlag, 1982), 68.

bodies, the eternal witnesses to this criminal act.

This morbid inclination opposes the structural aesthetic of French elegance to the aesthetic of softness. In the first category, one finds the modernist grid, to which belongs La Valise, a briefcase made from ABS plastic, designed by the Bouroullec brothers for Magis in 2003. Made troubling by its formal resemblance to a MacGuffin, La Valise seems to have been taken from an overly modernist 1950s drama, during an iconic scene of a document exchange, the acme of any self-respecting film noir. Such an object is a standard device in the quest for the document that haunts any spy story worthy of the name. The fact that the audience never sees the secret plans in Hitchcock's North by Northwest (1959) represents the ultimate success of the MacGuffin.

In contrast to the timeless dream of beautiful form, the aesthetic of softness in the 1970s is far more revolutionary. The design of Togo (1973), the bestselling sofa by Michel Ducaroy—who was inspired by the folds of a puffy tube of toothpaste that he found on the bathroom sink one morning—embodies the principle that "any precise form is the assassination of other versions."[24] As opposed to the rigidity of sofas designed a generation earlier, these qualities of the Togo reveal the displacement of the 1960s generation and formulate an ideological criticism of the second modernity.

Similar formal tensions accompanied the very inception of the design discipline. It was in this criminal mode that Sir Henry Cole, in 1852, opened the first museum of design and called it

[24] Carl Einstein, La ressemblance informe, ou le gai savoir visuel selon Georges Bataille (Paris: Macula, 1995), 186.

The Chamber of Horrors. Sir Henry—
head of the Royal Society for the
Encouragement of Arts, Manufactures
and Commerce; inventor and author,
in 1849, of the first published use of the
word "design" to indicate the creative
conception of manufactured objects;
founder of the Journal of Design and
Manufactures; and originator of the
Great Exhibition of 1851 in London—
gathered in his chamber eighty-seven
objects that would familiarize the
public with examples of bad taste,
in order that they might engage in
morally guided consumption.[25] A
century later, we still find the same
moral stakes in the twelve precepts of
"Good Design" enumerated by Edgar
Kaufman Jr.:

[Good design] should fulfill the
practical needs of modern life;
express the spirit of our times;

[25] See Christopher Frayling, Henry Cole and The Chamber of Horrors
(London: V&A, 2010).

benefit by contemporary advances
in the fine arts and pure sciences;
take advantage of new materials and
techniques and develop
familiar ones; develop forms,
textures and colors that spring
from the direct fulfillment of
requirements in appropriate
materials and techniques; express
the purpose of an object, never
making it to seem what it is not;
express the qualities and beauties
of the materials used, never making
the materials seem to be what
they are not; should express the
methods used to make an object,
not disguising mass production
as handicraft or simulating a
technique not used; lend the
expression of utility, materials
and process into a visually
satisfactory whole; be simple,
its structure, evident in its
appearance, avoiding extraneous
enrichment; master the machine

for the service of man; serve as wide a public as possible, considering modest needs and limited costs no less challenging than the requirements of pomp and luxury.[26]

The softness of the Togo, with its neighboring claims to pop culture, opposes these calls to virtuous good taste with camp, described by Susan Sontag as a "way of seeing the world as an aesthetic phenomenon...not in terms of beauty, but in terms of the degree of artifice, or stylization," and whose goal is to corrupt innocence.[27] With this move, the ideals of good taste have been hijacked and ruptured.

But the shelves of history, on which horrors have gathered together, cannot hide for long the spirits and other

[26] Edgar Kaufmann, Jr., What Is Modern Design? Introductory Series to the Modern Arts-3 (New York: MOMA, 1950), 7.
[27] Susan Sontag, "Notes on 'Camp'" (1964) in Art Theory and Criticism: An Anthology of Formalist, Avant-Garde, Contextualist and Post-Modern Thought, ed. Sally Everett (Jefferson, NC: McFarland & Company, 1991), 98, 102.

ghosts that haunt my investigation
into consumer goods and appliances.
Take the television in the 1982 film
Poltergeist by Tobe Hooper: telekinesis,
appearances, and disappearances
reveal the presence of the poltergeist,
which manifests itself brutally from
technological objects.

The impact on the imagination of
Roger Tallon's Téléavia P111,[28] a
portable television with retractable
handle that conceals the picture
tube within a smooth shell, can be
measured by the paradigm of the
nineteenth-century haunted house that
emerged concurrent with the advent of
technological devices. Aberrations of
nature, these haunted houses occupy
a space outside of the human realm,
a veritable embodiment of inhumanity.

[28] Raymond Guidot says Tallon was the first designer who, "to reduce eye fatigue
      of the user, placed in front of the cathode ray tube television sets...a screen
of colored polymethacrylate." [Raymond Guidot explique que Tallon fut le premier
designer qui 'pour diminuer la fatigue visuelle de l'utilisateur, plaça devant le tube
cathodique des postes de télévision...un écran de polyméthacrylate de méthyle
teinté.'], Histoire du design 1954–2000 (Paris: Hazan, 2000), 185.

The arrival of ghosts coincides with the introduction of invisible energies, such as gas and electricity, and echoes the anguish felt by those caught in the throes of this unprecedented domestic change. The Téléavia, with its tinted screen and its curved black surface, carries a stream of images, portable and mutable, spectral presences in black and white.

In Dark Places (2009), author Barry Curtis suggests that the supernatural acts as a symbol for forgetting, denial and perversion. The congruent appearance of ghosts and invisible energy suggests that the dark place of the human psyche responded to the discovery of radio waves in the 1880s by introducing the supernatural into the domestic sphere. The presence of invisible ghost technology has increased in parallel to the continued development of electronic devices. Curtis stipulated that, today,

"developments in miniaturization,
mobility and tele-presence and their
new kinds of 'magical' interface have
prompted new kinds of ghost
fictions....[29]" Elsa Frances'
Rock 'n' Rock, designed for the Tim
Thom department of Thomson,
anticipates an era in which nature is
never what it seems: masquerading
as a rock formation while carrying
invisible waves, this stereo system
is a bearer of phantoms.

[29] Barry Curtis, Dark Places (London: Reaktion Books, 2008), 22.

Home Sweet Ho(l)me(s):
The Joys of Crime at Home

Now it is time to figure out how the objects disappeared from the box that my future house from Starck came in. In this improbable speculation on French design, delightfully cluttered as it is with objects that are potentially criminal, that serve purposes other than those originally sanctioned, the history of design is changed. The publication of Pioneers of The Modern Movement by Pevsner first defined the professional, moral, and virtuous charge of the designer: the industrial production of good things. Yet at the very birth of the design discipline, with Sir Henry Cole's Chamber of Horrors, one already finds monstrosity, for the slightest deviation from Pevsner's principles has throughout the history of design been considered a criminal act.

In the present era, where the boundaries between disciplines are increasingly permeable, the designer attempts a few murders here and there. First, against the architect, appropriating domestic construction and everything associated with it in a declaration of independence, thereby transforming the home into a crime scene. Then, once the scene is set, the now murderous designer attempts to assassinate the past through appropriations of historic forms and the development of new ones. One is reminded here of De Quincey's connection of the dark matter of murder and the creation of art. The philosopher Vilém Flusser showed in his review of design and designers that design always involves a measure of treachery and perfidy, so that it then remains for one to decide "to be either a saint or a designer."[30]

[30] Vilém Flusser, Petite Philosophie du design (Paris: Circé, 2002), 32.
    ['Il faut se décider à être soit un saint, soit un designer.']

Audacity? A requirement for design? I fear that any understanding of the project is doomed to failure. I can only hope that this parallel between the activities of the first serial killer and French design, which takes for its premise an intrinsic link between modernity and crime, and more generally between designers and murderers, has taken you on a journey through a history of design that lies beyond function, and that can serve as a framework for a provisional hypothesis that I propose to leave open for a while yet. And if so, in this, the crime shall have been perfect!

PROJECT CONTRIBUTOR BIOGRAPHIES

matali crasset, an award-winning French industrial designer, is a graduate of Les Ateliers-Paris Design Institute (École nationale supérieure de création industrielle). She founded her own agency in 2000 after working with Philippe Starck. Her work is included in the Museum of Modern Art, New York; Musée des arts décoratifs, Paris; Centre Georges Pompidou; and the Centre national des arts plastiques (CNAP). Always in search of new territories to explore, she collaborates with eclectic worlds, from crafts to electronic music, from the hotel industry to trade fairs, realizing projects in set design, furniture, architecture, and graphics.

MARIANNE LAMONACA is the Associate Director for Curatorial Affairs and Education at The Wolfsonian–FIU. She has organized the exhibitions *A Bittersweet Decade: The New Deal in America, 1933–43*; *In Pursuit of Pleasure: Schultze & Weaver and the American Hotel*; *Print, Power, and Persuasion: Graphic Design in Germany, 1890–1945*; and *Tokyo: The Imperial Capital*, among many others. Her publications include *Grand Hotels of the Jazz Age: The Architecture of Schultze & Weaver*; "Whose History Is It Anyway? New Deal Murals in South Florida," in *A Paradigm for Progress: Art, Architecture, and the New Deal in South Florida*; and "A 'Return to Order': Issues of the Classical and the Vernacular in Italian Interwar Design," in *Designing Modernity: The Arts of Reform and Persuasion, 1885–1945*.

ALEXANDRA MIDAL is a freelance curator, design historian, and professor in history and theory of design and the head of the Masters in design at the University of Art & Design, Genève. A graduate of La Sorbonne, Paris and the School of Architecture at Princeton University, she served as director of the Regional Fund for Contemporary Art of Haute-Normandie (FRAC) and assistant to artist Dan Graham. She has curated numerous exhibitions, authored many articles, and written several books, including *Tomorrow Now: When Design Meets Science Fiction*; *Florence Doléac, climatologie domestique et cataclysmes émotionnels*; and *Design: Introduction à l'histoire d'une discipline*.

M/M (PARIS), founded in 1992, is a partnership between Mathias Augustyniak and Michael Amzalag. Working within the framework and language of design, they manifest a diverse practice across many cultural fields. They have been the subject of monographic exhibitions in the following institutions: Drawing Center, New York; Centre Pompidou, Paris; Palais de Tokyo, Paris; Frankfurter Kunstverein, Frankfurt. Their works are featured in public collections such as: Bibliothèque nationale de France, Paris; Centre Pompidou, Musée national d'art moderne, Paris; Design Museum, London; Fonds national d'art contemporain, Paris; Museum of Contemporary Art, Miami; MMK, Frankfurt; Museum für Gestaltung, Zürich; Musée d'art moderne de la ville de Paris; Stedelijk Museum, Amsterdam; Tate Modern, London; Vanabbe Museum, Eindhoven. Michael Amzalag studied at the École nationale supérieure des arts décoratifs, Paris, and Mathias Augustyniak studied at the Royal College of Arts, London.

EMILIA PHILIPPOT is the heritage curator for decorative art, craft, and industrial design at the Centre national des arts plastiques (CNAP). Prior to joining the CNAP, she was the heritage curator at the Réunion des musées nationaux (RMN). She jointly curated the exhibition *Warhol's Wide World* at the Galeries Nationales du Grand Palais in 2009 and co-wrote the catalogue *Le grand monde d'Andy* for the exhibition. Philippot has also contributed to a number of other publications, including *Masterpieces?* at the Centre Pompidou–Metz in 2010 and *Vilac, 100 Years of Wooden Toys* at the Musée des arts décoratifs, Paris in 2010.